Life Like

Summer Flowers

生·如·夏·花

泰戈尔经典诗选 I

[印] 泰戈尔 著
郑振铎 译

江苏凤凰文艺出版社
JIANGSU PHOENIX LITERATURE AND ART PUBLISHING LTD

新月集 | THE CRESCENT MOON | 001-121

目录

CONTENTS

目录

CONTENTS

新月集

THE CRESCENT MOON

家　庭

我独自在横跨过田地的路上走着，夕阳像一个守财奴似的，正藏起它最后的金子。

白昼更加深沉地没入黑暗之中，那已经收割了的孤寂的田地，默默地躺在那里。

天空里突然升起了一个男孩子尖锐的歌声。他穿过看不见的黑暗，留下他歌声的辙痕跨过黄昏的静谧。

他的乡村的家座落在荒凉的边上，在甘蔗田的后面，躲藏在香蕉树、瘦长的槟榔树、椰子树和深绿色的贾克果树的阴影里。

我在星光下独自走着的路上停留了一会，我看见黑沉沉的大地展开在我的面前，用她的手臂拥抱着无数的家庭，在那些家庭里有着摇篮和床铺，母亲们的心和夜晚的灯，还有年轻的生命，他们满心欢乐，却浑然不知这样的欢乐对于世界的价值。

THE HOME

I PACED alone on the road across the field while the sunset was hiding its last gold like a miser.

The daylight sank deeper and deeper into the darkness, and the widowed land, whose harvest had been reaped, lay silent.

Suddenly a boy' s shrill voice rose into the sky. He traversed the dark unseen, leaving the track of his song across the hush of the evening.

His village home lay there at the end of the waste land, beyond the sugarcane field, hidden among the shadows of the banana and the slender areca palm, the cocoanut and the dark green jack-fruit trees.

I stopped for a moment in my lonely way under the starlight, and saw spread before me the darkened earth surrounding with her arms countless homes furnished with cradles and beds, mothers' s hearts and evening lamps, and young lives glad with a gladness that knows nothing of its value for the world.

海　边

孩子们汇集在无边无际的世界的海边。

无垠的天穹静止地临于头上，不息的海水在足下汹涌。孩子们汇集在无边无际的世界的海边，叫着，跳着。

他们拿沙来建筑房屋，拿贝壳来做游戏。他们把落叶编成了船，笑嘻嘻地把它们放到大海上。孩子们在世界的海边，做他们的游戏。

他们不知道怎样泅水，他们不知道怎样撒网。采珠的人为了珠潜水，商人们在他们的船上航行，孩子们却只把小圆石聚了又散。他们不搜求宝藏，他们不知道怎样撒网。

大海哗笑着涌起波浪，而海滩的微笑荡漾着淡淡的光芒。致人死亡的波涛，对着孩子们唱无意义的歌曲，就像一个母亲在摇动她孩子的摇篮时一样。大海和孩子们一同游戏，而海滩的微笑荡漾着淡淡的光芒。

孩子们汇集在无边无际的世界的海边。狂风暴雨飘游在无辙迹的天空上，航船沉碎在无辙迹的海水里，死正在外面活动，孩子们却在游戏。无边无际的世界的海边，是孩子们的伟大聚会所。

ON THE SEASHORE

ON the seashore of endless worlds children meet. The infinite sky is motionless overhead and the restless water is boisterous. On the seashore of endless worlds the children meet with shouts and dances.

They build their houses with sand, and they play with empty shells. With withered leaves they weave their boats and smilingly float them on the vast deep. Children have their play on the seashore of worlds.

They know not how to swim, they know not how to cast nets. Pearl-fishers dive for pearls, merchants sail in their ships, while children gather pebbles and scatter them again. They seek not for hidden treasures, they know not how to cast nets.

The sea surges up with laughter, and pale gleams the smile of the sea-beach. Death-dealing waves sing meaningless ballads to the children, even like a mother while rocking her baby' s cradle. The sea plays with children, and pale gleams the smile of the sea-beach.

On the seashore of endless worlds children meet. Tempest roams in the pathless sky, ships are wrecked in the trackless water, death is abroad and children play. On the seashore of endless worlds is the great meeting of children.

来 源

流泛在孩子两眼的睡眠——有谁知道它是从什么地方来的？是的，有个谣传，说它是住在萤火虫朦胧地照耀着林荫的仙村里，在那个地方，挂着两个迷人的胆怯的蓓蕾。它便是从那个地方来吻了孩子的两眼的。

当孩子睡时，在他唇上浮动着的微笑——有谁知道它是从什么地方生出来的？是的，有个谣传，说新月的一线年轻的清光，触着将消未消的秋云边上，于是微笑便初生在一个浴在清露里的早晨的梦中了——当孩子睡时，微笑便在他的唇上浮动着。

甜蜜柔嫩的新鲜生气，像花一般地在孩子的四肢上开放着——有谁知道它在什么地方藏得这样久？是的，当妈妈还是一个少女的时候，它已在爱的温柔而沉静的神秘中，潜伏在她的心里了——甜蜜柔嫩的新鲜生气，像花一般地在孩子的四肢上开放着。

THE SOURCE

THE sleep that flits on baby' s eyes — does anybody know from where it comes? Yes, there is a rumour that it has its dwelling where, in the fairy village among shadows of the forest dimly lit with glow-worms, there hang two shy buds of enchantment. From there it comes to kiss baby' s eyes.

The smile that flickers on baby' s lips when he sleeps — does anybody know where it was born? Yes, there is a rumour that a young pale beam of a crescent moon touched the edge of a vanishing autumn cloud, and there the smile was first born in the dream of a dew-washed morning — the smile that flickers on baby' s lips when he sleeps.

The sweet, soft freshness that blooms on baby' s limbs — does anybody know where it was hidden so long? Yes, when the mother was a young girl it lay pervading her heart in tender and silent mystery of love — the sweet, soft freshness that has bloomed on baby' s limbs.

孩童之道

只要孩子愿意，他此刻便可飞上天去。

他所以不离开我们，并不是没有缘故。

他爱把他的头倚在妈妈的胸间，他即使是一刻不见她，也是不行的。

孩子知道各式各样的聪明话，虽然世间的人很少懂得这些话的意义。

他所以永不想说，并不是没有缘故。

他所要做的一件事，就是要学习从妈妈的嘴唇里说出来的话，那就是他所以看来这样天真的缘故。

孩子有成堆的黄金与珠子，但他到这个世界上来，却像一个乞丐。

他所以这样假装了来，并不是没有缘故。

这个可爱的小小的裸着身体的乞丐，所以假装着完全无助的样子，便是想要乞求妈妈的爱的财富。

孩子在纤小的新月的世界里，是一切束缚都没有的。

他所以放弃了他的自由，并不是没有缘故。

他知道有无穷的快乐藏在妈妈的心的小小一隅里，被妈妈亲爱的手臂所拥抱，其甜美远胜过自由。

孩子永不知道如何哭泣，他所住的是完全的乐土。

他所以要流泪，并不是没有缘故。

虽然他用了可爱的脸上的微笑，引逗得他妈妈热切的心向着他，然而他因为细故而发的小小的哭声，却编成了怜与爱双重约束的带子。

BABY' S WAY

IF baby only wanted to, he could fly up to heaven this moment.

It is not for nothing that he does not leave us.

He loves to rest his head on mother' s bosom, and cannot ever bear to lose sight of her.

Baby knows all manner of wise words, though few on earth can understand their meaning.

It is not for nothing that he never wants to speak.

The one thing he wants is to learn mother's words from mother' s lips. That is why he looks so innocent.

Baby had a heap of gold and pearls, yet he came like a beggar on to this earth.

It is not for nothing he came in such a disguise.

This dear little naked mendicant pretends to be utterly helpless, so that he may beg for mother' s wealth of love.

Baby was so free from every tie in the land of the tiny crescent moon.

It was not for nothing he gave up his freedom.

He knows that there is room for endless joy in mother' s little corner of a heart, and it is sweeter far than liberty to be caught and pressed in her dear arms.

Baby never knew how to cry. He dwelt in the land of perfect bliss.

It is not for nothing he has chosen to shed tears.

Though with the smile of his dear face he draws mother' s yearning heart to him, yet his little cries over tiny troubles weave the double bond of pity and love.

不被注意的花饰

啊，谁给那件小外衫染上颜色的，我的孩子，谁使你的温软的肢体穿上那件红的小外衫的？

你在早晨就跑出来到天井里玩儿，你，跑着就像摇摇欲跌似的。

但是谁给那件小外衫染上颜色的，我的孩子？

什么事叫你大笑起来的，我的小小的命芽儿？

妈妈站在门边，微笑地望着你。

她拍着她的双手，她的手镯丁当地响着，你手里拿着你的竹竿儿在跳舞，活像一个小小的牧童。

但是什么事叫你大笑起来的，我的小小的命芽儿？

喔，乞丐，你双手攀搂住妈妈的头颈，要乞讨些什么？

喔，贪得无厌的心，要我把整个世界从天上摘下来，像摘一个果子似的，把它放在你那一双小小的玫瑰色的手掌上吗？

喔，乞丐，你要乞讨些什么？

风高兴地带走了你踝铃的丁当。

太阳微笑着，望着你的打扮。

当你睡在你妈妈的臂弯里时，天空在上面望着你，而早晨蹑手蹑脚地走到你的床跟前，吻着你的双眼。

风高兴地带走了你踝铃的丁当。

仙乡里的梦婆飞过朦胧的天空，向你飞来。

在你妈妈的心头上，那世界母亲正和你坐在一块儿。

他，向星星奏乐的人，正拿着他的横笛，站在你的窗边。

仙乡里的梦婆飞过朦胧的天空，向你飞来。

THE UNHEEDED PAGEANT

AH, who was it coloured that little frock, my child, and covered your sweet limbs with that little red tunic?

You have come out in the morning to play in the courtyard, tottering and tumbling as you run.

But who was it coloured that little frock, my child?

What is it makes you laugh, my little life-bud?

Mother smiles at you standing on the threshold.

She claps her hands and her bracelets jingle, and you dance with your bamboo stick in your hand like a tiny little shepherd.

But what is it makes you laugh, my little life-bud?

O beggar, what do you beg for, clinging to your mother' s neck with both your hands?

O greedy heart, shall I pluck the world like a fruit from the sky to place it on your little rosy palm?

O beggar, what are you begging for?

The wind carries away in glee the tinkling of your anklet bells.

The sun smiles and watches your toilet. The sky watches over you when you sleep in your mother' s arms, and the morning comes tiptoe to your bed and kisses your eyes.

The wind carries away in glee the tinkling of your anklet bells.

The fairy mistress of dreams is coming towards you, flying through the twilight sky.

The world-mother keeps her seat by you in your mother's heart.

He who plays his music to the stars is standing at your window with his flute.

And the fairy mistress of dreams is coming towards you, flying through the twilight sky.

偷睡眠者

谁从孩子的眼里把睡眠偷了去呢？我一定要知道。

妈妈把她的水罐挟在腰间，走到近村汲水去了。

这是正午的时候，孩子们游戏的时间已经过去了；池中的鸭子沉默无声。

牧童躺在榕树的荫下睡着了。

白鹤庄重而安静地立在檬果树边的泥泽里。

就在这个时候，偷睡眠者跑来从孩子的两眼里捉住睡眠，便飞去了。

当妈妈回来时，她看见孩子四肢着地在屋里爬着。

谁从孩子的眼里把睡眠偷了去呢？我一定要知道。我一定要找到她，把她锁起来。

我一定要向那个黑洞里张望，在这个洞里，有一道小泉从圆的和有皱纹的石上滴下来。

我一定要到醉花[1]林中的沉寂的树影里搜寻，在这林中，鸽子在它们住的地方咕咕地叫着，仙女的脚环在繁星满天的静夜里丁当地响着。

我要在黄昏时，向静静的萧萧的竹林里窥望，在这林中，萤火虫闪闪地耗费它们的光明，只要遇见一个人，我便要问他：“谁能告诉我，偷睡眠者住在什么地方？”

谁从孩子的眼里把睡眠偷了去呢？我一定要知道。

只要我能捉住她，怕不会给她一顿好教训！

我要闯入她的巢穴，看她把所有偷来的睡眠藏在什么地方。

我要把它都夺来，带回家去。

我要把她的双翼缚得紧紧的，把她放在河边，然后叫她拿一根芦苇在灯心草和睡莲间钓鱼为戏。

黄昏，街上已经收了市，村里的孩子们都坐在妈妈的膝上时，夜鸟便会讥笑地在她耳边说：

“你现在还想偷谁的睡眠呢？”

①醉花（bakula），学名 Mimusops Elengi。印度传说美女口中吐出香液，此花始开。

SLEEP-STEALER

WHO stole sleep from baby's eyes? I must know.

Clasping her pitcher to her waist mother went to fetch water from the village nearby.

It was noon. The children's playtime was over; the ducks in the pond were silent.

The shepherd boy lay asleep under the shadow of the banyan tree.

The crane stood grave and still in the swamp near the mango grove.

In the meanwhile the Sleep-stealer came and, snatching sleep from baby's eyes, flew away.

When mother came back she found baby travelling the room over on all fours.

Who stole sleep from our baby's eyes? I must know. I must find her and chain her up.

I must look into that dark cave, where, through boulders and scowling stones, trickles a tiny stream.

I must search in the drowsy shade of the bakula grove, where pigeons coo in their corner, and fairies' anklets tinkle in the stillness of starry nights.

In the evening I will peep into the whispering silence of the bamboo forest, where fireflies squander their light, and will ask every creature I meet, "Can anybody tell me where the Sleep-stealer lives?"

Who stole sleep from baby' s eyes? I must know.

Shouldn' t I give her a good lesson if I could only catch her!

I would raid her nest and see where she hoards all her stolen sleep.

I would plunder it all, and carry it home.

I would bind her two wings securely, set her on the bank of the river, and then let her play at fishing with a reed among the rushes and water-lilies.

When the marketing is over in the evening, and the village children sit in their mothers' laps, then the night birds will mockingly din her ears with:

"Whose sleep will you steal now?"

开　始

“我是从哪儿来的，你，在哪儿把我捡起来的？”孩子问他的妈妈说。

她把孩子紧紧地搂在胸前，半哭半笑地答道——

“你曾被我当作心愿藏在我的心里，我的宝贝。

“你曾存在于我孩童时代玩的泥娃娃身上；每天早晨我用泥土塑造我的神像，那时我反复地塑了又捏碎了的就是你。

“你曾和我们的家庭守护神一同受到祀奉，我崇拜家神时也就崇拜了你。

“你曾活在我所有的希望和爱情里，活在我的生命里，我母亲的生命里。

“在主宰着我们家庭的不死的精灵的膝上，你已经被抚育了好多代了。

“当我做女孩子的时候，我心的花瓣儿张开，你就像一股花香似的散发出来。

“你软软的温柔，在我的青春的肢体上开花了，像太阳出来之前的天空上的一片曙光。

“上天的第一宠儿，晨曦的孪生兄弟，你从世界的生命的溪流浮泛而下，终于停泊在我的心头。

“当我凝视你的脸蛋的时候，神秘之感淹没了我；你这属于一切人的，竟成了我的。

“为了怕失掉你，我把你紧紧地搂在胸前。是什么魔术把这世界的宝贝引到我这双纤小的手臂里来呢？”

THE BEGINNING

"WHERE have I come from, where did you pick me up?" the baby asked its mother.

She answered half crying, half laughing, and clasping the baby to her breast, — "You were hidden in my heart as its desire, my darling.

You were in the dolls of my childhood' s games; and when with clay I made the image of my god every morning, I made and unmade you then.

You were enshrined with our household deity, in his worship I worshipped you.

In all my hopes and my loves, in my life, in the life of my mother you have lived.

In the lap of the deathless Spirit who rules our home you have been nursed for ages.

When in girlhood my heart was opening its petals, you hovered as a fragrance about it.

Your tender softness bloomed in my youthful limbs, like a glow in the sky before the sunrise.

Heaven' s first darling, twin-born with the morning light, you have floated down the stream of the world' s life, and at last you have stranded on my heart.

As I gaze on your face, mystery overwhelms me; you who belong to all have become mine.

For fear of losing you I hold you tight to my breast. What magic has snared the world' s treasure in these slender arms of mine?"

孩子的世界

我愿我能在我孩子自己的世界的中心，占一角清净地。

我知道有星星同他说话，天空也在他面前垂下，用它傻傻的云朵和彩虹来娱悦他。

那些大家以为他是哑的人，那些看去像是永不会走动的人，都带了他们的故事，捧了装满五颜六色的玩具的盘子，匍匐地来到他的窗前。

我愿我能在横过孩子心中的道路上游行，解脱一切的束缚；

在那儿，使者奉了无所谓的使命奔走于无史的诸王的王国间；

在那儿，理智以她的法律造为纸鸢而飞放，真理也使事实从桎梏中自由了。

BABY'S WORLD

I WISH I could take a quiet corner in the heart of my baby' s very own world.

I know it has stars that talk to him, and a sky that stoops down to his face to amuse him with its silly clouds and rainbows.

Those who make believe to be dumb, and look as if they never could move, come creeping to his window with their stories and with trays crowded with bright toys.

I wish I could travel by the road that crosses baby' s mind, and out beyond all bounds;

Where messengers run errands for no cause between the kingdoms of kings of no history;

Where Reason makes kites of her laws and flies them, and Truth sets Fact free from its fetters.

时候与原因

当我给你五颜六色的玩具的时候，我的孩子，我明白了为什么云上、水上是这样的色彩缤纷，为什么花朵上染上绚烂的颜色的原因了——当我给你五颜六色的玩具的时候，我的孩子。

当我唱着使你跳舞的时候，我真的知道了为什么树叶响着音乐，为什么波浪把它们合唱的声音送进静听着的大地的心头的原因了——当我唱着使你跳舞的时候。

当我把糖果送到你贪得无厌的双手上的时候，我知道了为什么花萼里会有蜜，为什么水果里会秘密地充溢了甜汁的原因了——当我把糖果送到你贪得无厌的双手上的时候。

当我吻着你的脸蛋儿叫你微笑的时候，我的宝贝，我的确明白了在晨光里、从天上流下来的是什么样的快乐，而夏天的微风吹拂在我的身体上又是什么样的爽快——当我吻着你的脸蛋儿叫你微笑的时候。

WHEN AND WHY

WHEN I bring you coloured toys, my child, I understand why there is such a play of colours on clouds, on water, and why flowers are painted in tints — when I give coloured toys to you, my child.

When I sing to make you dance, I truly know why there is music in leaves, and why waves send their chorus of voices to the heart of the listening earth — when I sing to make you dance.

When I bring sweet things to your greedy hands, I know why there is honey in the cup of the flower, and why fruits are secretly filled with sweet juice — when I bring sweet things to your greedy hands.

When I kiss your face to make you smile, my darling, I surely understand what pleasure streams from the sky in morning light, and what delight the summer breeze brings to my body — when I kiss you to make you smile.

责　备

为什么你眼里有了眼泪，我的孩子？

他们真是可怕，常常无谓地责备你！

你写字时，墨水玷污了你的手和脸——这就是他们所以骂你龌龊的缘故吗？

呵，呸！他们也敢因为圆圆的月儿用墨水涂了脸，便骂它龌龊吗？

他们总要为了每一件小事去责备你，我的孩子。他们总是无谓地寻人错处。

你游戏时扯破了你的衣服——这就是他们所以说你不整洁的缘故吗？

呵，呸！秋之晨从它破碎的云衣中露出微笑。那么，他们要叫它什么呢？

他们对你说什么话，尽管可以不去理睬他，我的孩子。

他们把你做错的事儿长长地记了一笔账。

谁都知道你是十分喜欢糖果的——这就是他们所以称你贪婪的缘故吗？

呵，呸！我们是喜欢你的，那么，他们要叫我们什么呢？

DEFAMATION

WHY are those tears in your eyes, my child?

How horrid of them to be always scolding you for nothing?

You have stained your fingers and face with ink while writing — is that why they call you dirty?

O, fie! Would they dare to call the full moon dirty because it has smudged its face with ink?

For every little trifle they blame you, my child. They are ready to find fault for nothing.

You tore your clothes while playing — is that why they call you untidy?

O, fie! What would they call an autumn morning that smiles through its ragged clouds?

Take no heed of what they say to you, my child.

Take no heed of what they say to you, my child.

They make a long list of your misdeeds. Everybody knows how you love sweet things — is that why they call you greedy?

O, fie! What then would they call us who love you?

审判官

你想说他什么尽管说吧，但是我知道我孩子的短处。

我爱他并不因为他好，只是因为他是我的小小的孩子。

你如果把他的好处与坏处两两相权一下，恐怕你就会知道他是如何的可爱吧?

当我必须责罚他的时候，他更成为我生命的一部分了。

当我使他眼泪流出时，我的心也和他同哭了。

只有我才有权去骂他，去责罚他，因为只有热爱人的才可以惩戒人。

THE JUDGE

SAY of him what you please, but I know my child' s failings.

I do not love him because he is good, but because he is my little child.

How should you know how dear he can be when you try to weigh his merits against his faults?

When I must punish him he becomes all the more a part of my being.

When I cause his tears to come my heart weeps with him.

I alone have a right to blame and punish, for he only may chastise who loves.

玩　具

孩子，你真是快活呀，一早晨坐在泥土里，玩着折下来的小树枝儿。

我微笑地看你在那里玩着那根折下来的小树枝儿。

我正忙着算账，一小时一小时地在那里叠加数字。

也许你在看我，想道："这种好没趣的游戏，竟把你的一早晨的好时间浪费掉了！"

孩子，我忘了聚精会神玩耍树枝与泥饼的方法了。

我寻求贵重的玩具，收集金块与银块。

你呢，无论找到什么便去做你快乐的游戏，我呢，却把我的时间与力气都浪费在那些我永不能得到的东西上。

我在我脆薄的独木船里挣扎着要航过欲望之海，竟忘了我也是在那里做游戏了。

PLAYTHINGS

CHILD, how happy you are sitting in the dust, playing with a broken twig all the morning.

I smile at your play with that little bit of a broken twig.

I am busy with my accounts, adding up figures by the hour.

Perhaps you glance at me and think, "What a stupid game to spoil your morning with!"

Child, I have forgotten the art of being absorbed in sticks and mud-pies.

I seek out costly playthings, and gather lumps of gold and silver.

With whatever you find you create your glad games, I spend both my time and my strength over things I never can obtain.

In my frail canoe I struggle to cross the sea of desire, and forget that I too am playing a game.

天文家

我不过说："当傍晚圆圆的满月挂在迦昙波①的枝头时，有人能去捉住它吗？"

哥哥却对我笑道："孩子呀，你真是我所见到的最傻的孩子。月亮离我们这样远，谁能去捉住它呢？"

我说："哥哥，你真傻！当妈妈向窗外探望，微笑着往下看我们游戏时，你也能说她远吗？"

哥哥还是说："你这个傻孩子！但是，孩子，你到哪里去找一个大得能逮住月亮的网呢？"

我说："你自然可以用双手去捉住它呀。"

但是哥哥还是笑着说："你真是我所见到的最傻的孩子！如果月亮走近了，你便知道它是多么大了。"

我说："哥哥，你们学校里所教的，真是没有用呀！当妈妈低下脸儿跟我们亲嘴时，她的脸看来也是很大的吗？"

但是哥哥还是说："你真是一个傻孩子。"

①迦昙波，原名 Kadam，亦作 Kadamba，学名 Namlea Cadamba，意译"白花"，即昙花。

THE ASTRONOMER

I ONLY said, "When in the evening the round full moon gets entangled among the branches of that Kadam tree, couldn' t somebody catch it?"

But dada [elder brother] laughed at me and said, "Baby, you are the silliest child I have ever known. The moon is ever so far from us, how could anybody catch it?"

I said, "Dada how foolish you are! When mother looks out of her window and smiles down at us playing, would you call her far away?"

Still said, "You are a stupid child! But, baby, where could you find a net big enough to catch the moon with?"

I said, "Surely you could catch it with your hands."

But dada laughed and said, "You are the silliest child I have known. If it came nearer, you would see how big the moon is."

I said, "Dada, what nonsense they teach at your school! When mother bends her face down to kiss us does her face look very big?"

But still dada says, "You are a stupid child."

云与波

妈妈，住在云端的人对我唤道——

“我们从醒的时候游戏到白日终止。

“我们与金黄色的曙光游戏，我们与银白色的月亮游戏。”

我问道：“但是，我怎么能够上你那里去呢？”

他们答道：“你到地球的边上来，举手向天，就可以被接到云端里来了。”

“我妈妈在家里等我呢，”我说，“我怎么能离开她而来呢？”

于是他们微笑着浮游而去。

但是我知道一件比这个更好的游戏，妈妈。

我做云，你做月亮。

我用两只手遮盖你，我们的屋顶就是青碧的天空。

住在波浪上的人对我唤道——

“我们从早晨唱歌到晚上；我们前进又前进的旅行，也不知我们所经过的是什么地方。”

我问道：“但是，我怎么能加入你们队

伍里去呢？”

他们告诉我说：“来到岸旁，站在那里，紧闭你的两眼，你就被带到波浪上来了。”

我说：“傍晚的时候，我妈妈常要我在家里——我怎么能离开她而去呢！”

于是他们微笑着，跳舞着奔流过去。

但是我知道一件比这个更好的游戏。

我是波浪，你是陌生的岸。

我奔流而进，进，进，笑哈哈地撞碎在你的膝上。

世界上就没有一个人会知道我们俩在什么地方。

CLOUDS AND WAVES

MOTHER, the folk who live up in the clouds call out to me —

"We play from the time we wake till the day ends.

We play with the golden dawn, we play with the silver moon."

I ask, "But, how am I to get up to you?" They answer, "Come to the edge of the earth, lift up your hands to the sky, and you will be taken up into the clouds."

"My mother is waiting for me at home," I say. "How can I leave her and come?"

Then they smile and float away.

But I know a nicer game than that, mother.

I shall be the cloud and you the moon.

I shall cover you with both my hands, and our house-top will be the blue sky.

The folk who live in the waves call out to me —

"We sing from morning till night; on and on we travel and know not where we pass."

I ask, "But, how am I to join you?" They tell me, "Come to the edge of the shore and stand with your eyes tight shut, and you will be carried out upon the waves."

I say, "My mother always wants me at home in the evening — how can I leave her and go?"

Then they smile, dance and pass by.

But I know a better game than that.

I will be the waves and you will be a strange shore.

I shall roll on and on and on, and break upon your lap with laughter.

And no one in the world will know where we both are.

金色花

假如我变成了一朵金色花[1]，只是为了好玩，长在那棵树的高枝上，笑哈哈地在风中摇摆，又在新生的树叶上跳舞，妈妈，你会认识我吗?

你要是叫道：“孩子，你在哪里呀？”我暗暗地在那里偷笑，却一声儿不响。

我要悄悄地开放花瓣儿，看着你工作。

当你沐浴后，湿发披在两肩，穿过金色花的林荫，走到你做祷告的小庭院时，你会嗅到这花的香气，却不知道这香气是从我身上来的。

当你吃过中饭，坐在窗前读《罗摩衍那》[2]，那棵树的阴影落在你的头发与膝上时，我便要投我的小小的影子在你的书页上，正投在你所读的地方。

但是你会猜得出这就是你的小孩子的小影子吗?

当你黄昏时拿了灯到牛棚里去，我便要突然地再落到地上来，又成了你的孩子，求你讲个故事给我听。

“你到哪里去了，你这坏孩子？”

“我不告诉你，妈妈。”这就是你同我那时所要说的话了。

①金色花，原名champa，亦作Champak，学名Michelia Champaca，印度圣树，木兰花属植物，开金黄色碎花。译名亦作“瞻波伽”或“占博迦”。

②《罗摩衍那》（Ramayana）为印度叙事诗，相传系蚁垤（Valmiki）所作。今传本形式约为公元二世纪间所形成。全书分为七卷，共二万四千颂，皆系叙述罗摩生平之作。罗摩即罗摩犍陀罗。十车王之子，悉多之夫。他于第二世（Treta yaga）入世，为毗湿奴神第七化身。印人看他为英雄，崇拜他如神。

THE CHAMPA FLOWER

SUPPOSING I became a champa flower, just for fun, and grew on a branch high up that tree, and shook in the wind with laughter and danced upon the newly budded leaves, would you know me, mother?

You would call, "Baby, where are you?" and I should laugh to myself and keep quite quiet.

I should slyly open my petals and watch you at your work.

When after your bath, with wet hair spread on your shoulders, you walked through the shadow of the champa tree to the little court where you say your prayers, you would notice the scent of the flower, but not know that it came from me.

When after the midday meal you sat at the window reading Ramayana, and the tree' s shadow fell over your hair and your lap, I should fling my wee little shadow on to the page of your book, just where you were reading.

But would you guess that it was the tiny shadow of your little child?

When in the evening you went to the cow-shed with the lighted lamp in your hand, I should suddenly drop on to the earth again and be your own baby once more, and beg you to tell me a story.

"Where have you been, you naughty child?"

"I won' t tell you, mother." That' s what you and I would say then.

仙人世界

如果人们知道了我的国王的宫殿在哪里，它就会消失在空气中的。

墙壁是白色的银，屋顶是耀眼的黄金。

皇后住在有七个庭院的宫苑里，她戴的一串珠宝，值得整整七个王国的全部财富。

不过，让我悄悄地告诉你，妈妈，我的国王的宫殿究竟在哪里。

它就在我们阳台的角上，在那栽着杜尔茜花的花盆放着的地方。

公主躺在远远的、隔着七个不可逾越重洋的那一岸沉睡着。

除了我自己，世界上便没有人能够找到她。

她臂上有镯子，她耳上挂着珍珠，她的头发拖到地板上。

当我用我的魔杖点触她的时候，她就会醒过来，而当她微笑时，珠玉将会从她唇边落下来。

不过，让我在你的耳朵边悄悄地告诉你，妈妈，她就住在我们阳台的角上，在那栽着杜尔茜花的花盆放着的地方。

当你要到河里洗澡的时候，你走上屋顶的那座阳台来吧。

我就坐在墙的阴影所聚会的一个角落里。

我只让小猫儿跟我在一起，因为它知道那故事里的理发匠住的地方。

不过，让我在你的耳朵边悄悄地告诉你，那故事里的理发匠到底住在哪里。

他住的地方就在阳台的角上，在那栽着杜尔茜花的花盆放着的地方。

FAIRYLAND

IF people came to know where my king' s palace is, it would vanish into the air.The walls are of white silver and the roof of shining gold.

The queen lives in a palace with seven courtyards, and she wears a jewel that cost all the wealth of seven kingdoms.

But let me tell you, mother, in a whisper, where my king' s palace is.

It is at the corner of our terrace where the pot of the tulsi plant stands.

The princess lies sleeping on the far-away shore of the seven impassable seas.

There is none in the world who can find her but myself.

She has bracelets on her arms and pearl drops in her ears; her hair sweeps down upon the floor.

She will wake when I touch her with my magic wand, and jewels will fall from her lips when she smiles.

But let me whisper in your ear, mother; she is there in the corner of our terrace where the pot of the tulsi plant stands.

When it is time for you to go to the river for your bath, step up to that terrace on the roof.I sit in the corner where the shadows of the walls meet together.

Only puss is allowed to come with me, for she knows where the barber in the story lives.

But let me whisper, mother, in your ear where the barber in the story lives.

It is at the corner of the terrace where the pot of the tulsi plant stands.

流放的地方

妈妈，天空上的光成灰色了，我不知道是什么时候了。

我玩得怪没劲儿的，所以到你这里来了。这是星期六，是我们的休息日。

放下你的活计，妈妈，坐在靠窗的一边，告诉我，童话里的特潘塔沙漠在什么地方？

雨的影子遮掩了整个白天。

凶猛的电光用它的爪子抓着天空。

当乌云在轰轰地响着，天打着雷的时候，我总爱心里带着恐惧爬伏到你的身上。

当大雨倾泻在竹叶子上好几个钟头，而我们的窗户被狂风震得格格发响的时候，我就爱独自和你坐在屋里，妈妈，听你讲童话里的特潘塔沙漠的故事。

它在哪里？妈妈，在哪一个海洋的岸上，在哪些个山峰的脚下，在哪一个国王的国土里？

田地上没有此疆彼壤的界石，也没有村人在黄昏时走回家的，或妇人在树林里捡拾枯枝而捆载到市场上去的道路。沙地上只有一小块儿黄色草地，只有一棵树，就是那一对聪明的老鸟儿在那里做窝的，那个地方就是特潘塔沙漠。

我能够想象得到，就在这样一个乌云密布的日子，国王年轻的儿子，怎样地独自骑着一匹灰色马，走过这个沙漠，去寻找那被囚禁在不可知的重洋之外的巨人宫里的公主。

当雨雾在遥远的天空下降，电光像一阵突然发作的痛楚痉挛似的闪射的时候，他可记得他不幸的母亲，为国王所弃，正在扫除牛棚，眼里流着眼泪，当他骑马走过童话里的特潘塔沙漠的时候？

看，妈妈，一天还没有完，天色就差不多黑了，那边村庄的路上没有什么旅客了。

牧童早就从牧场上回家了，人们都已从田地里回来，坐在他们草屋的檐下的草席上，眼望着阴沉的云块。

妈妈，我把我所有的书本都放在书架上了——不要叫我现在做功课。

当我长大了，大得像爸爸一样的时候，我将会学到必须学的东西。

但是，今天你可得告诉我，妈妈，童话里的特潘塔沙漠在什么地方？

THE LAND OF THE EXILE

MOTHER, the light has grown grey in the sky; I do not know what the time is.

There is no fun in my play, so I have come to you. It is Saturday, our holiday.

Leave off your work, mother; sit here by the window and tell me where the desert of Tepantar in the fairy tale is?

The shadow of the rains has covered the day from end to end.

The fierce lightning is scratching the sky with its nails.

When the clouds rumble and it thunders, I love to be afraid in my heart and cling to you.

When the heavy rain patters for hours on the bamboo leaves, and our windows shake and rattle at the gusts of wind, I like to sit alone in the room, mother, with you, and hear you talk about the desert of Tepantar in the fairy tale.

Where is it, mother, on the shore of what sea, at the foot of what hills, in the kingdom of what king?

There are no hedges there to mark the fields, no footpath across it by which the villagers reach their village in the evening, or the woman who gathers dry sticks in the forest can bring her load to the market.

With patches of yellow grass in the sand and only one tree where the pair of wise old birds have their nest, lies the desert of Tepantar.

I can imagine how, on just such a cloudy day, the young son of the king is riding alone on a grey horse through the desert, in search of the princess who lies imprisoned in the giant' s palace across that unknown water.

When the haze of the rain comes down in the distant sky, and lightning starts up like a sudden fit of pain, does he remember his unhappy mother, abandoned by the king, sweeping the cow-stall and wiping her eyes, while he rides through the desert of Tepantar in the fairy tale?

See, mother, it is almost dark before the day is over, and there are no travellers yonder on the village road.

The shepherd boy has gone home early from the pasture, and men have left their fields to sit on mats under the eaves of their huts, watching the scowling clouds.

Mother, I have left all my books on the shelf — do not ask me to do my lessons now.

When I grow up and am big like my father, I shall learn all that must be learnt.

But just for today, tell me, mother, where the desert of Tepantar in the fairy tale is?

雨 天

乌云很快地集拢在森林的黝黑的边缘上。

孩子，不要出去呀！

湖边的一行棕树，向暝暗的天空撞着头；羽毛零乱的乌鸦，静悄悄地栖在罗望子的枝上，河的东岸正被乌沉沉的暝色所侵袭。

我们的牛系在篱上，高声鸣叫。

孩子，在这里等着，等我先把牛牵进牛棚里去。

许多人都挤在池水泛溢的田间，捉那从泛溢的池中逃出来的鱼儿，雨水成了小河，流过狭街，好像一个嬉笑的孩子从他妈妈那里跑开，故意要恼她一样。

听呀，有人在浅滩上喊船夫呢。

孩子，天色暝暗了，渡头的摆渡船已经停了。

天空好像是在滂沱的雨上快跑着；河里的水喧叫而且暴躁；妇人们早已拿着汲满了水的水罐，从恒河畔匆匆地回家了。

夜里用的灯，一定要预备好。

孩子，不要出去呀！

到市场去的大道已没有人走，到河边去的小路又很滑。风在竹林里咆哮着，挣扎着，好像一只落在网中的野兽。

THE RAINY DAY

SULLEN clouds are gathering fast over the black fringe of the forest.

O child, do not go out!

The palm trees in a row by the lake are smiting their heads against the dismal sky; the crows with their draggled wings are silent on the tamarind branches, and the eastern bank of the river is haunted by a deepening gloom.

Our cow is lowing loud, tied at the fence.

O child, wait here till I bring her into the stall.

Men have crowded into the flooded field to catch the fishes as they escape from the overflowing ponds; the rain water is running in rills through the narrow lanes like a laughing boy who has run away from his mother to tease her.

Listen, someone is shouting for the boatman at the ford.

O child, the daylight is dim, and the crossing at the ferry is closed.

The sky seems to ride fast upon the madly-rushing rain; the water in the river is loud and impatient; women have hastened home early from the Ganges with their filled pitchers.

The evening lamps must be made ready.

O child, do not go out!

The road to the market is desolate, the lane to the river is slippery. The wind is roaring and struggling among the bamboo branches like a wild beast tangled in a net.

纸　船

我每天把纸船一个个放在急流的溪中。

我用大黑字写我的名字和我住的村名在纸船上。

我希望住在异地的人会得到这纸船，知道我是谁。

我把园中长的秀利花载在我的小船上，希望这些黎明开的花能在夜里被平平安安地带到岸上。

我投我的纸船到水里，仰望天空，看见小朵的云正张着满鼓着风的白帆。

我不知道天上有我的什么游伴把这些船放下来同我的船比赛！

夜来了，我的脸埋在手臂里，梦见我的纸船在子夜的星光下缓缓地浮泛前去。

睡仙坐在船里，带着满载着梦的篮子。

PAPER BOATS

DAY by day I float my paper boats one by one down the running stream.

In big black letters I write my name on them and the name of the village where I live.

I hope that someone in some strange land will find them and know who I am.

I load my little boats with shiuli flowers from our garden, and hope that these blooms of the dawn will be carried safely to land in the night.

I launch my paper boats and look up into the sky and see the little clouds setting their white bulging sails.

I know not what playmate of mine in the sky sends them down the air to race with my boats!

When night comes I bury my face in my arms and dream that my paper boats float on and on under the midnight stars.

The fairies of sleep are sailing in them, and the lading is their baskets full of dreams.

水　手

船夫曼特胡的船只停泊在拉琪根琪码头。

这只船无用地装载着黄麻，无所事事地停泊在那里已经好久了。

只要他肯把他的船借给我，我就给它安装一百只桨，扬起五个或六个或七个布帆来。

我决不把它驾驶到愚蠢的市场上去。

我将航行遍仙人世界里的七个大海和十三条河道。

但是，妈妈，你不要躲在角落里为我哭泣。

我不会像罗摩犍陀罗[①]似的，到森林中去，一去十四年才回来。

我将成为故事中的王子，把我的船装满了我所喜欢的东西。

我将带我的朋友阿细和我做伴，我们要快快乐乐地航行于仙人世界里的七个大海和十三条河道。

我将在绝早的晨光里张帆航行。

中午，你正在池塘里洗澡的时候，我们将在一个陌生的国王的国土上了。

我们将经过特浦尼浅滩，把特潘塔沙漠抛落在我们的后边。

当我们回来的时候，天色快黑了，我将告诉你，我们所见到的一切。

我将越过仙人世界里的七个大海和十三条河道。

①罗摩犍陀罗即罗摩。他是印度叙事诗《罗摩衍那》中的主角。为了尊重父亲的诺言和维持弟兄间的友爱，他抛弃了继承王位的权利，和妻子悉多在森林中被放逐了十四年。

THE SAILOR

THE boat of the boatman Madhu is moored at the wharf of Rajgunj.

It is uselessly laden with jute, and has been lying there idle for ever so long.

If he would only lend me his boat, I should man her with a hundred oars, and hoist sails, five or six or seven.

I should never steer her to stupid markets. I should sail the seven seas and the thirteen rivers of fairyland.

But, mother, you won't weep for me in a corner.

I am not going into the forest like Ramachandra to come back only after fourteen years.

I shall become the prince of the story, and fill my boat with whatever I like.

I shall take my friend Ashu with me. We shall sail merrily across the seven seas and the thirteen rivers of fairyland.

We shall set sail in the early morning light.

When at noontide you are bathing at the pond, we shall be in the land of a strange king.

We shall pass the ford of Tirpurni, and leave behind us the desert of Tepantar.

When we come back it will be getting dark, and I shall tell you of all that we have seen.

I shall cross the seven seas and the thirteen rivers of fairyland.

对　岸

我渴想到河的对岸去。

在那边，好些船只一行儿系在竹竿上；

人们在早晨乘船渡过那边去，肩上扛着犁头，去耕耘他们远处的田；

在那边，牧人使他们鸣叫着的牛游泳到河旁的牧场去；

黄昏的时候，他们都回家了，只留下豺狼在这满长着野草的岛上哀叫。

妈妈，如果你不在意，我长大的时候，要做这渡船的船夫。

据说有好些古怪的池塘藏在这个高岸之后。

雨过去了，一群一群的野鹜飞到那里去，茂盛的芦苇在岸边四围生长，水鸟在那里生蛋；

竹鸡带着跳舞的尾巴，将它们细小的足印印在洁净的软泥上；

黄昏的时候，长草顶着白花，邀月光在长草的波浪上浮游。

妈妈，如果你不在意，我长大的时候，要做这渡船的船夫。

我要自此岸至彼岸，渡过来，渡过去，所有村中正在那儿沐浴的男孩女孩，都要诧异地望着我。

太阳升到中天，早晨变为正午了，我将跑到你那里去，说道：“妈妈，我饿了！”

一天完了，影子俯伏在树底下，我便要在黄昏中回家来。

我将永不同爸爸那样，离开你到城里去做事。

妈妈，如果你不在意，我长大的时候，要做这渡船的船夫。

THE FURTHER BANK

I LONG to go over there to the further bank of the river,

Where those boats are tied to the bamboo poles in a line;

Where men cross over in their boats in the morning with ploughs on their shoulders to till their far-away fields;

Where the cowherds make their lowing cattle swim across to the riverside pasture;

Whence they all come back home in the evening, leaving the jackals to howl in the island overgrown with weeds,

Mother, if you don' t mind, I should like to become the boatman of the ferry when I am grown up.

They say there are strange pools hidden behind that high bank,

Where flocks of wild ducks come when the rains are over, and thick reeds grow round the margins where waterbirds lay their eggs;

Where snipes with their dancing tails stamp their tiny footprints upon the clean soft mud;

Where in the evening the tall grasses crested with white flowers invite the moonbeam to float upon their waves.

Mother, if you don' t mind, I should like to become the boatman of the ferryboat when I am grown up.

I shall cross and cross back from bank to bank, and all the boys and girls of the village will wonder at me while they are bathing.

When the sun climbs the mid sky and morning wears on to noon, I shall come running to you, saying, "Mother, I am hungry!"

When the day is done and the shadows cower under the trees, I shall come back in the dusk.

I shall never go away from you into the town to work like father.

Mother, if you don' t mind, I should like to become the boatman of the ferryboat when I am grown up.

花的学校

当雷云在天上轰响，六月的阵雨落下的时候，

润湿的东风走过荒野，在竹林中吹着口笛。

于是一群一群的花从无人知道的地方突然跑出来，在绿草上狂欢地跳着舞。

妈妈，我真的觉得那群花朵是在地下的学校里上学。

它们关了门做功课，如果它们想在散学以前出来游戏，它们的老师是要罚它们站墙角的。

雨一来，它们便放假了。

树枝在林中互相碰触着，绿叶在狂风里萧萧地响着，雷云拍着大手，花孩子们便在那时候穿了紫的、黄的、白的衣裳，冲了出来。

你可知道，妈妈，它们的家是在天上，在星星所住的地方。

你没有看见它们怎样地急着要到那儿去吗？你不知道它们为什么那样急急忙忙吗？

我自然能够猜得出它们是对谁扬起双臂来：它们也有它们的妈妈，就像我有我自己的妈妈一样。

THE FLOWER-SCHOOL

WHEN storm clouds rumble in the sky and June showers come down,

The moist east wind comes marching over the heath to blow its bagpipes among the bamboos.

Then crowds of flowers come out of a sudden, from nobody knows where, and dance upon the grass in wild glee.

Mother, I really think the flowers go to school underground.

They do their lessons with doors shut, and if they want to come out to play before it is time, their master makes them stand in a corner.

When the rains come they have their holidays.

Branches clash together in the forest, and the leaves rustle in the wild wind, the thunder-clouds clap their giant hands and the flower children rush out in dresses of pink and yellow and white.

Do you know, mother, their home is in the sky, where the stars are.

Haven' t you seen how eager they are to get there? Don' t you know why they are in such a hurry?

Of course, I can guess to whom they raise their arms: they have their mother as I have my own.

商　人

妈妈，让我们想象，你待在家里，我到异邦去旅行。再想象，我的船已经装得满满的在码头上等候启航了。

现在，妈妈，好好想一想再告诉我，回来的时候我要带些什么给你。

妈妈，你要一堆一堆的黄金吗？在金河的两岸，田野里全是金色的稻实。在林荫的路上，金色花也一朵一朵地落在地上。

我要为你把它们全都收拾起来，放在好几百个篮子里。

妈妈，你要秋天的雨点一般大的珍珠吗？我要渡海到珍珠岛的岸上去。那个地方，在清晨的曙光里，珠子在草地的野花上颤动，珠子落在绿草上，珠子被汹狂的海浪一大把一大把地撒在沙滩上。我的哥哥呢，我要送他一对有翼的马，会在云端飞翔的。

爸爸呢，我要带一支有魔力的笔给他，他还没有察觉，笔就写出字来了。你呢，妈妈，我一定要把那个值七个王国的首饰箱和珠宝送给你。

THE MERCHANT

IMAGINE, mother, that you are to stay at home and I am to travel into strange lands.

Imagine that my boat is ready at the landing fully laden.

Now think well, mother, before you say what I shall bring for you when I come back.

Mother, do you want heaps and heaps of gold?

There, by the banks of golden streams, fields are full of golden harvest.

And in the shade of the forest path the golden champa flowers drop on the ground.

I will gather them all for you in many hundred baskets.

Mother, do you want pearls big as the raindrops of autumn?

I shall cross to the pearl island shore. There in the early morning light pearls tremble on the meadow flowers, pearls drop on the grass, and pearls are scattered on the sand in spray by the wild sea-waves.

My brother shall have a pair of horses with wings to fly among the clouds.

For father I shall bring a magic pen that, without his knowing, will write of itself.

For you, mother, I must have the casket and jewel that cost seven kings their kingdoms.

同　情

如果我只是一只小狗，而不是你的小孩，亲爱的妈妈，当我想吃你盘里的东西时，你要向我说“不”吗？

你要赶开我，对我说道“滚开，你这淘气的小狗”吗？

那么，走吧，妈妈，走吧！当你叫唤我的时候，我就永不到你那里去，也永不要你再喂我吃东西了。

如果我只是一只绿色的小鹦鹉，而不是你的小孩，亲爱的妈妈，你要把我紧紧地锁住，怕我飞走吗？

你要对我摇你的手，说道：“怎样的一个不知感恩的贱鸟呀！整夜地尽在咬它的链子吗？”

那么，走吧，妈妈，走吧！我要跑到树林里去，我就永不再让你抱我在你的臂里了。

SYMPATHY

IF I were only a little puppy, not your baby, mother dear, would you say "No" to me if I tried to eat from your dish?

Would you drive me off, saying to me, "Get away, you naughty little puppy?"

Then go, mother, go! I will never come to you when you call me, and never let you feed me any more.

If I were only a little green parrot, and not your baby, mother dear, would you keep me chained lest I should fly away?

Would you shake your finger at me and say, "What an ungrateful wretch of a bird! It is gnawing at its chain day and night?"

Then, go, mother, go! I will run away into the woods; I will never let you take me in your arms again.

职　业

早晨，钟敲十下的时候，我沿着我们的小巷到学校去。

每天我都遇见那个小贩，他叫道："镯子呀，亮晶晶的镯子！"

他没有什么事情急着要做，他没有哪条街一定要走，他没有什么地方一定要去，他没有什么时间一定要回家。

我愿意我是一个小贩，在街上过日子，叫着："镯子呀，亮晶晶的镯子！"

下午四点，我从学校里回家。

从一家门口，我看见一个园丁在那里掘地。

他用他的锄子，要怎么掘，便怎么掘，他被尘土污了衣裳，如果他被太阳晒黑了或是身上被打湿了，都没有人骂他。

我愿意我是一个园丁，在花园里掘地，谁也不来阻止我。

天色刚黑，妈妈就送我上床。

从开着的窗口，我看见更夫走来走去。

小巷又黑又冷清，路灯立在那里，像一

个头上生着一只红眼睛的巨人。

更夫摇着他的提灯，跟他身边的影子一起走着，他一生一次都没有上床去过。

我愿意我是一个更夫，整夜在街上走，提了灯去追逐影子。

VOCATION

WHEN the gong sounds ten in the morning and I walk to school by our lane,

Every day I meet the hawker crying, "Bangles, crystal bangles!"

There is nothing to hurry him on, there is no road he must take, no place he must go to, no time when he must come home.

I wish I were a hawker, spending my day in the road, crying, "Bangles, crystal bangles!"

When at four in the afternoon I come back from the school,

I can see through the gate of that house the gardener digging the ground.

He does what he likes with his spade, he soils his clothes with dust, nobody takes him to task if he gets baked in the sun or gets wet.

I wish I were a gardener digging away at the garden with nobody to stop me from digging.

Just as it gets dark in the evening and my mother sends me to bed,

I can see through my open window the watchman walking up and down.

The lane is dark and lonely, and the street-lamp stands like a giant with one red eye in its head.

The watchman swings his lantern and walks with his shadow at his side, and never once goes to bed in his life.

I wish I were a watchman walking the streets all night, chasing the shadows with my lantern.

长　者

妈妈，你的孩子真傻！她是那么可笑的不懂事！

她不知道路灯和星星的分别。

当我们玩着把小石子当食物的游戏时，她便以为它们真是吃的东西，竟想放进嘴里去。

当我翻开一本书，放在她面前，要她读 a，b，c 时，她却用手把书页撕了，无端快活地叫起来，你的孩子就是这样做功课的。

当我生气地对她摇头，骂她，说她顽皮时，她却哈哈大笑，以为很有趣。

谁都知道爸爸不在家，但是，如果我在游戏时高声叫一声“爸爸”，她便要高兴地四面张望，以为爸爸真是近在身边。

当我把洗衣人带来载衣服回去的驴子当作学生，并且警告她说，我是老师，她却无缘无故地乱叫起我哥哥来。

你的孩子要捉月亮。

她是这样的可笑；她把格尼许[1]唤作琪奴许。

妈妈，你的孩子真傻，她是那么可笑的不懂事！

①格尼许（ganesh）是毁灭之神湿婆的儿子，象首人身。同时也是现代印度人所最喜欢用来做名字的第一个字。

SUPERIOR

MOTHER, your baby is silly! She is so absurdly childish!

She does not know the difference between the lights in the streets and the stars.

When we play at eating with pebbles, she thinks they are real food, and tries to put them into her mouth.

When I open a book before her and ask her to learn her a, b, c, she tears the leaves with her hands and roars for joy at nothing; this is your baby' s way of doing her lesson.

When I shake my head at her in anger and scold her and call her naughty, she laughs and thinks it great fun.

Everybody knows that father is away, but if in play I call aloud "Father," she looks about her in excitement and thinks that father is near.

When I hold my class with the donkeys that our washerman brings to carry away the clothes and I warn her that I am the schoolmaster, she will scream for no reason and call me dada. [elder brother].

Your baby wants to catch the moon. She is so funny; she calls Ganesh Ganush. [Ganesh, a common name in India, also that of the god with the elephant' s head.]

Mother, your baby is silly, she is so absurdly childish!

小大人

我人很小，因为我是一个小孩子，到了我像爸爸一样年纪时，便要变大了。

我的先生要是走来说道："时候晚了，把你的石板、你的书拿来。"

我便要告诉他道："你不知道我已经同爸爸一样大了吗？

我决不再学什么功课了。"

我的老师便将惊异地说道："他读书不读书可以随便，因为他是大人了。"

我将自己穿了衣裳，走到人群拥挤的市场里去。

我的叔叔要是跑过来说道："你要迷路了，我的孩子，让我领着你吧。"

我便要回答道："你没有看见吗，叔叔，我已经同爸爸一样大了？我决定要独自一个人到市场里去。"

叔叔便将说道："是的，他随便到哪里去都可以，因为他是大人了。"

当我正拿钱给我保姆时，妈妈便要从浴室中出来，因为我是知道怎样用我的钥匙去开银箱的。

妈妈要是说道：“你在做什么呀，顽皮的孩子？”

我便要告诉她道：“妈妈，你不知道我已经同爸爸一样大了吗？我必须拿钱给保姆。”

妈妈便将自言自语道：“他可以随便把钱给他所喜欢的人，因为他是大人了。”

当十月里放假的时候，爸爸将要回家，他会以为我还是一个小孩子，为我从城里带了小鞋子和小绸衫来。

我便要说道：“爸爸，把这些东西给哥哥吧，因为我已经同你一样大了。”

爸爸便将想了一想，说道：“他可以随便去买他自己穿的衣裳，因为他是大人了。”

THE LITTLE BIG MAN

I AM small because I am a little child. I shall be big when I am as old as my father is.

My teacher will come and say, "It is late, bring your slate and your books."

I shall tell him, "Do you not know I am as big as father? And I must not have lessons any more."

My master will wonder and say, "He can leave his books if he likes, for he is grown up."

I shall dress myself and walk to the fair where the crowd is thick.

My uncle will come rushing up to me and say, "You will get lost, my boy; let me carry you."

I shall answer, "Can' t you see, uncle, I am as big as father. I must go to the fair alone."

Uncle will say, "Yes, he can go wherever he likes, for he is grown up."

Mother will come from her bath when I am giving money to my nurse, for I shall know how to open the box with my key.

Mother will say, "What are you about, naughty child?"

I shall tell her, "Mother, don' t you know, I am as big as father, and I must give silver to my nurse."

Mother will say to herself, "He can give money to whom he likes, for he is grown up."

In the holiday time in October father will come home and, thinking that I am still a baby, will bring for me from the town little shoes and small silken frocks.

I shall say, "Father, give them to my dada [elder brother], for I am as big as you are."

Father will think and say, "He can buy his own clothes if he likes, for he is grown up."

十二点钟

妈妈，我真想现在不做功课了，我整个早晨都在念书呢。

你说，现在还不过是十二点钟。假定不会晚过十二点吧；难道你不能把不过是十二点钟想象成下午吗？

我能够容易地想象：现在太阳已经到了那片稻田的边缘上了，老态龙钟的渔婆正在池边采撷香草做她的晚餐。

我闭上了眼就能够想到，马塔尔树下的阴影更深黑了，池塘里的水看来黑得发亮。

假如十二点钟能够在黑夜里来到，为什么黑夜不能在十二点钟的时候来到呢？

TWELVE O' CLOCK

MOTHER, I do want to leave off my lessons now. I have been at my book all the morning.

You say it is only twelve o' clock. Suppose it isn' t any later; can' t you ever think it is afternoon when it is only twelve o' clock?

I can easily imagine now that the sun has reached the edge of that rice-field, and the old fisher-woman is gathering herbs for her supper by the side of the pond.

I can just shut my eyes and think that the shadows are growing darker under the madar tree, and the water in the pond looks shiny black.

If twelve o' clock can come in the night, why can' t the night come when it is twelve o' clock?

著作家

你说爸爸写了许多书，但我却不懂得他所写的东西。

他整个黄昏读书给你听，但是你真懂得他的意思吗？

妈妈，你给我们讲的故事，真是好听呀！我很奇怪，爸爸为什么不能写那样的书呢？

难道他从来没有从他自己的妈妈那里听见过巨人和神仙和公主的故事吗？

还是已经完全忘记了？

他常常耽误了沐浴，你不得不走去叫他一百多次。

你总要等候着，把他的菜温着等他，但他忘了，还尽管写下去。

爸爸老是以著书为游戏。

如果我一走进爸爸房里去游戏，你就要走来叫道："真是一个顽皮的孩子！"

如果我稍微出一点声音，你就要说："你没有看见你爸爸正在工作吗？"

老是写了又写，有什么趣味呢？

当我拿起爸爸的钢笔或铅笔，像他一模

一样地在他的书上写着a，b，c，d，e，f，g，h，i——那时，你为什么跟我生气呢，妈妈？

爸爸写时，你却从来不说一句话。

当我爸爸耗费了那么一大堆纸时，妈妈，你似乎全不在乎。

但是，如果我只取了一张纸去做一只船，你却要说："孩子，你真讨厌！"

你对于爸爸拿黑点子涂满了纸的两面，污损了许多许多张纸，你心里以为怎样呢？

AUTHORSHIP

YOU say that father writes a lot of books, but what he writes I don't understand.

He was reading to you all the evening, but could you really make out what he meant?

What nice stories, mother, you can tell us! Why can't father write like that, I wonder?

Did he never hear from his own mother stories of giants and fairies and princesses?

Has he forgotten them all?

Often when he gets late for his bath you have to go and call him an hundred times.

You wait and keep his dishes warm for him, but he goes on writing and forgets.

Father always plays at making books.

If ever I go to play in father's room, you come and call me, "what a naughty child!"

If I make the slightest noise, you say, "Don't you see that father's at his work?"

What's the fun of always writing and writing?

When I take up father's pen or pencil and write upon his book just as he does, — a, b, c, d, e, f, g, h, i, — why do you get cross with me, then, mother?

You never say a word when father writes.

When my father wastes such heaps of paper, mother, you don't seem to mind at all.

But if I take only one sheet to make a boat with, you say, "Child, how troublesome you are!"

What do you think of father's spoiling sheets and sheets of paper with black marks all over on both sides?

恶邮差

你为什么坐在那边地板上不言不语的，告诉我呀，亲爱的妈妈？

雨从开着的窗口打进来了，把你身上全打湿了，你却不管。

你听见钟已打四下了吗？正是哥哥从学校里回家的时候了。

到底发生了什么事，你的神色这样不对？

你今天没有接到爸爸的信吗？

我看见邮差在他的袋里带了许多信来，几乎镇里的每个人都分送到了。

只有爸爸的信，他留起来给他自己看。我确信这个邮差是个坏人。

但是不要因此不开心呀，亲爱的妈妈。

明天是邻村市集的日子，你叫女仆去买些笔和纸来。

我自己会写爸爸所写的一切信，使你找不出一点错处来。

我要从 A 字一直写到 K 字。

但是，妈妈，你为什么笑呢？

你不相信我能写得同爸爸一样好！

但是我将用心画格子，把所有的字母都写得又大又美。

当我写好了时，你以为我也像爸爸那样傻，把它投入可怕的邮差的袋中吗？

我立刻就自己送来给你，而且一个字母、一个字母地帮助你读。

我知道那邮差是不肯把真正的好信送给你的。

THE WICKED POSTMAN

WHY do you sit there on the floor so quiet and silent, tell me, mother dear?

The rain is coming in through the open window, making you all wet, and you don' t mind it.

Do you hear the gong striking four? It is time for my brother to come home from school.

What has happened to you that you look so strange?

Haven' t you got a letter from father today?

I saw the postman bringing letters in his bag for almost everybody in the town.

Only, father' s letters he keeps to read himself. I am sure the postman is a wicked man.

But don' t be unhappy about that, mother dear.

Tomorrow is market day in the next village. You ask your maid to buy some pens and papers.

I myself will write all father's letters; you will not find a single mistake.

I shall write from A right up to K.

But, mother, why do you smile?

You don' t believe that I can write as nicely as father does!

But I shall rule my paper carefully, and write all the letters beautifully big.

When I finish my writing, do you think I shall be so foolish as father and drop it into the horrid postman's bag?

I shall bring it to you myself without waiting, and letter by letter help you to read my writing.

I know the postman does not like to give you the really nice letters.

英　雄

妈妈，让我们想象我们正在旅行，经过一个陌生而危险的国土。

你坐在一顶轿子里，我骑着一匹红马，在你旁边跑着。

是黄昏的时候，太阳已经下山了。约拉地希的荒地疲乏而灰暗地展开在我们面前。大地是凄凉而荒芜的。

你害怕了，心想："我不知道我们到了什么地方了。"

我对你说道："妈妈，不要害怕。"

草地上刺蓬蓬地长着针尖似的草，一条狭而崎岖的小道通过这块草地。

在这片广大的地面上看不见一只牛，它们已经回到它们村里的牛棚去了。

天色黑了下来，大地和天空都显得朦朦胧胧的，而我们不能说出我们正走向什么所在。

突然间，你叫我，悄悄地问我道："靠近河岸的是什么火光呀？"

正在那个时候，一阵可怕的呐喊声爆发了，好些人影向我们跑过来。

你蹲坐在你的轿子里，嘴里反复地祷念

着神的名字。

轿夫们，怕得发抖，躲藏在荆棘丛中。

我向你喊道："不要害怕，妈妈，有我在这里。"

他们手里执着长棒，头发披散着，越走越近了。

我喊道："要当心！你们这些坏蛋！再向前走一步，你们就要送命了。"

他们又发出一阵可怕的呐喊声，向前冲过来。

你抓住我的手，说道："好孩子，看在上天面上，躲开他们吧。"

我说道："妈妈，你瞧我的。"

于是我刺策着我的马匹，猛奔过去，我的剑和盾彼此碰着作响。

这一场战斗是那么激烈，妈妈，如果你从轿子里看得见的话，你一定会发冷战的。

他们之中，许多人逃走了，还有好些人被砍杀了。

我知道你那时独自坐在那里，心里正在想着，你的孩子这时候一定已经死了。

但是我跑到你的跟前，浑身溅满了鲜血，说道："妈妈，现在战争已经结束了。"

你从轿子里走出来，吻着我，把我搂在你的心头，你自言自语地说道：

"如果我没有我的孩子护送我，我简直不知道怎么办才好。"

一千件无聊的事天天在发生，为什么这样一件事不能够偶然实现呢？

这很像一本书里的一个故事。

我的哥哥要说道："这是可能的事吗？我老是在想，他是那么嫩弱呢！"

我们村里的人们都要惊讶地说道："这孩子正和他妈妈在一起，这不是很幸运吗？"

THE HERO

MOTHER, let us imagine we are travelling, and passing through a strange and dangerous country.

You are riding in a palanquin and I am trotting by you on a red horse.

It is evening and the sun goes down. The waste of Joradighi lies wan and grey before us. The land is desolate and barren.

You are frightened and thinking — "I know not where we have come to."

I say to you, "Mother, do not be afraid."

The meadow is prickly with spiky grass, and through it runs a narrow broken path.

There are no cattle to be seen in the wide field; they have gone to their village stalls.

It grows dark and dim on the land and sky, and we cannot tell where we are going.

Suddenly you call me and ask me in a whisper, "What light is that near the bank?"

Just then there bursts out a fearful yell, and figures come running towards us.

You sit crouched in your palanquin and repeat the names of the gods in prayer.

The bearers, shaking in terror, hide themselves in the thorny bush.

I shout to you, "Don' t be afraid, mother. I am here."

With long sticks in their hands and hair all wild about their heads, they come nearer and nearer.

I shout, "Have a care! you villains! One step more and you are dead men."

They give another terrible yell and rush forward.

You clutch my hand and say, "Dear boy, for heaven' s sake, keep away from them."

I say, "Mother, just you watch me."

Then I spur my horse for a wild gallop, and my sword and buckler clash against each other.

The fight becomes so fearful, mother, that it would give you a cold shudder could you see it from your palanquin.

Many of them fly, and a great number are cut to pieces.

I know you are thinking, sitting all by yourself, that your boy must be dead by this time.

But I come to you all stained with blood, and say, "Mother, the fight is over now."

You come out and kiss me, pressing me to your heart, and you say to yourself,

"I don' t know what I should do if I hadn' t my boy to escort me."

A thousand useless things happen day after day, and why couldn't such a thing come true by chance?

It would be like a story in a book.

My brother would say, "Is it possible? I always thought he was so delicate!"

Our village people would all say in amazement, "Was it not lucky that the boy was with his mother?"

告　别

是我走的时候了，妈妈，我走了。

当清寂的黎明，你在暗中伸出双臂，要抱你睡在床上的孩子时，我要说道："孩子不在那里呀！"——妈妈，我走了。

我要变成一股清风抚摸着你；我要变成水的涟漪，当你浴时，把你吻了又吻。

大风之夜，当雨点在树叶中淅沥时，你在床上，会听见我的微语，当电光从开着的窗口闪进你的屋里时，我的笑声也偕了它一同闪进了。

如果你醒着躺在床上，想你的孩子到深夜，我便要从星空向你唱道："睡呀！妈妈，睡呀。"

我要坐在各处游荡的月光上，偷偷地来到你的床上，乘你睡着时，躺在你的胸上。

我要变成一个梦儿，从你的眼皮的微缝中，钻到你睡眠的深处。当你醒来吃惊地四望时，我便如闪耀的萤火似的熠熠地向暗中飞去了。

当普耶节日①，邻舍家的孩子们来屋里游玩时，我便要融化在笛声里，整日在你心头震荡。

亲爱的阿姨带了普耶礼[2]来，问道："我们的孩子在哪里，姊姊？"妈妈，你将要柔声地告诉她："他呀，他现在是在我的瞳仁里，他现在是在我的身体里，在我的灵魂里。"

①普耶（puja），意为"祭神大典"，这里的"普耶节"，是指印度十月间的"难近母祭日"。

②普耶礼就是指这个节日亲友相互馈送的礼物。

THE END

IT is time for me to go, mother; I am going.

When in the paling darkness of the lonely dawn you stretch out your arms for your baby in the bed, I shall say, "Baby is not there!" — mother, I am going.

I shall become a delicate draught of air and caress you; and I shall be ripples in the water when you bathe, and kiss you and kiss you again.

In the gusty night when the rain patters on the leaves you will hear my whisper in your bed, and my laughter will flash with the lightning through the open window into your room.

If you lie awake, thinking of your baby till late into the night, I shall sing to you from the stars, "Sleep mother, sleep."

On the straying moonbeams I shall steal over your bed, and lie upon your bosom while you sleep.

I shall become a dream, and through the little opening of your eyelids I shall slip into the depths of your sleep; and when you wake up and look round startled, like a twinkling firefly I shall flit out into the darkness.

When, on the great festival of puja, the neighbours' children come and play about the house, I shall melt into the music of the flute and throb in your heart all day.

Dear auntie will come with puja-presents and will ask, "Where is our baby, sister? " Mother, you will tell her softly, "He is in the pupils of my eyes, he is in my body and in my soul."

召　唤

她走的时候，夜间黑漆漆的，他们都睡了。

现在，夜间也是黑漆漆的，我唤她道：“回来，我的宝贝；世界都在沉睡，当星星互相凝视的时候，你来一会儿是没有人会知道的。”

她走的时候，树木正在萌芽，春光刚刚来到。

现在花已盛开，我唤道：“回来，我的宝贝。孩子们漫不经心地在游戏，把花聚在一起，又把它们散开。你如走来，拿一朵小花去，没有人会发觉的。”

常常在游戏的那些人，仍然还在那里游戏，生命总是如此的浪费。

我静听他们的空谈，便唤道：“回来，我的宝贝，妈妈的心里充满着爱，你如走来，仅仅从她那里接一个小小的吻，没有人会妒忌的。”

THE RECALL

THE night was dark when she went away, and they slept.

The night is dark now, and I call for her, "Come back, my darling; the world is asleep; and no one would know, if you came for a moment while stars are gazing at stars."

She went away when the trees were in bud and the spring was young.

Now the flowers are in high bloom and I call, "Come back, my darling. The children gather and scatter flowers in reckless sport. And if you come and take one little blossom no one will miss it."

Those that used to play are playing still, so spendthrift is life.

I listen to their chatter and call, "Come back, my darling, for mother' s heart is full to the brim with love, and if you come to snatch only one little kiss from her no one will grudge it."

第一次的茉莉

呵，这些茉莉花，这些白的茉莉花！

我仿佛记得我第一次双手满捧着这些茉莉花，这些白的茉莉花的时候。

我喜爱那日光，那天空，那绿色的大地；

我听见那河水淙淙的流声，在黑漆的午夜里传过来；

秋天的夕阳，在荒原上大路转角处迎我，如新妇揭起她的面纱迎接她的爱人。

但我想起孩提时第一次捧在手里的白茉莉，心里充满着甜蜜的回忆。

我生平有过许多快活的日子，在节日宴会的晚上，我曾跟着说笑话的人大笑。

在灰暗的雨天的早晨，我吟哦过许多飘逸的诗篇。

我颈上戴过爱人手织的醉花的花圈，作为晚装。

但我想起孩提时第一次捧在手里的白茉莉，心里充满着甜蜜的回忆。

THE FIRST JASMINES

AH, these jasmines, these white jasmines!

I seem to remember the first day when I filled my hands with these jasmines, these white jasmines.

I have loved the sunlight, the sky and the green earth;

I have heard the liquid murmur of the river through the darkness of midnight;

Autumn sunsets have come to me at the bend of a road in the lonely waste, like a bride raising her veil to accept her lover.

Yet my memory is still sweet with the first white jasmines that I held in my hand when I was a child.

Many a glad day has come in my life, and I have laughed with merrymakers on festival nights.

On grey mornings of rain I have crooned many an idle song.

I have worn round my neck the evening wreath of bakulas woven by the hand of love.

Yet my heart is sweet with the memory of the first fresh jasmines that filled my hands when I was a child.

榕 树

喂，你站在池边的蓬头的榕树，你可会忘记了那小小的孩子，就像那在你的枝上筑巢又离开了你的鸟儿似的孩子?

你不记得他是怎样坐在窗内，诧异地望着你深入地下的纠缠的树根吗?

妇人们常到池边，汲了满罐的水去，你的大黑影便在水面上摇动，好像睡着的人挣扎着要醒来似的。

日光在微波上跳舞，好像从不停息的小梭在织着金色的花毡。

两只鸭子挨着芦苇，在芦苇影子上游来游去，孩子静静地坐在那里想着。

他想做风，吹过你的萧萧的枝杈；想做你的影子，在水面上，随了日光而俱长；想做一只鸟儿，栖息在你的最高枝上；还想做那两只鸭子，在芦苇与阴影中间游来游去。

THE BANYAN TREE

O YOU shaggy-headed banyan tree standing on the bank of the pond, have you forgotten the little child, like the birds that have nested in your branches and left you?

Do you not remember how he sat at the window and wondered at the tangle of your roots that plunged underground?

The women would come to fill their jars in the pond, and your huge black shadow would wriggle on the water like sleep struggling to wake up.

Sunlight danced on the ripples like restless tiny shuttles weaving golden tapestry.

Two ducks swam by the weedy margin above their shadows, and the child would sit still and think.

He longed to be the wind and blow through your rustling branches, to be your shadow and lengthen with the day on the water, to be a bird and perch on your top-most twig, and to float like those ducks among the weeds and shadows.

祝　福

祝福这个小心灵，这个洁白的灵魂，他为我们的大地，赢得了天的接吻。

他爱日光，他爱见他妈妈的脸。

他没有学会厌恶尘土而渴求黄金。

紧抱他在你的心里，并且祝福他。

他已来到这个歧路百出的大地上了。

我不知道他怎么从群众中选出你来，来到你的门前抓住你的手问路。

他笑着，谈着，跟着你走，心里没有一点儿疑惑。

不要辜负他的信任，引导他到正路，并且祝福他。

把你的手按在他的头上，祈求着：底下的波涛虽然险恶，然而从上面来的风，会鼓起他的船帆，送他到和平的港口。

不要在忙碌中把他忘了，让他来到你的心里，并且祝福他。

BENEDICTION

BLESS this little heart, this white soul that has won the kiss of heaven for our earth.

He loves the light of the sun, he loves the sight of his mother' s face.

He has not learned to despise the dust, and to hanker after gold.

Clasp him to your heart and bless him.

He has come into this land of an hundred cross-roads.

I know not how he chose you from the crowd, came to your door, and grasped your hand to ask his way.

He will follow you, laughing and talking, and not a doubt in his heart.

Keep his trust, lead him straight and bless him.

Lay your hand on his head, and pray that though the waves underneath grow threatening, yet the breath from above may come and fill his sails and waft him to the haven of peace.

Forget him not in your hurry, let him come to your heart and bless him.

赠品

我要送些东西给你，我的孩子，因为我们同是漂泊在世界的溪流中。

我们的生命将被分开，我们的爱也将被忘记。

但我却没有那样傻，希望能用我的赠品来买你的心。

你的生命正是青青，你的道路也长着呢，你一口气饮尽了我们带给你的爱，便回身离开我们跑了。

你有你的游戏，有你的游伴。如果你没有时间同我们在一起，如果你想不到我们，那有什么害处呢？

我们呢，自然的，在老年时，会有许多闲暇的时间，去计算那过去的日子，把我们手里永久失了的东西，在心里爱抚着。

河流唱着歌很快地流去，冲破所有的堤防。但是山峰却留在那里，忆念着，满怀依依之情。

THE GIFT

I WANT to give you something, my child, for we are drifting in the stream of the world.

Our lives will be carried apart, and our love forgotten.

But I am not so foolish as to hope that I could buy your heart with my gifts.

Young is your life, your path long, and you drink the love we bring you at one draught and turn and run away from us.

You have your play and your playmates. What harm is there if you have no time or thought for us.

We, indeed, have leisure enough in old age to count the days that are past, to cherish in our hearts what our hands have lost for ever.

The river runs swift with a song, breaking through all barriers. But the mountain stays and remembers, and follows her with his love.

我的歌

我的孩子，我这一支歌将扬起它的乐声围绕你的身旁，好像那爱情的热恋的手臂一样。

我这一支歌将触着你的前额，好像那祝福的接吻一样。

当你只是一个人的时候，它将坐在你的身旁，在你耳边微语着；当你在人群中的时候，它将围住你，使你超然物外。

我的歌将成为你的梦的翼翅，它将把你的心移送到不可知的岸边。

当黑夜覆盖在你路上的时候，它又将成为那照临在你头上忠实的星光。

我的歌又将坐在你眼睛的瞳仁里，将你的视线带入万物的心里。

当我的声音因死亡而沉寂时，我的歌仍将在你活泼的心中唱着。

MY SONG

THIS song of mine will wind its music around you, my child, like the fond arms of love.

This song of mine will touch your forehead like a kiss of blessing.

When you are alone it will sit by your side and whisper in your ear, when you are in the crowd it will fence you about with aloofness.

My song will be like a pair of wings to your dreams, it will transport your heart to the verge of the unknown.

It will be like the faithful star overhead when dark night is over your road.

My song will sit in the pupils of your eyes, and will carry your sight into the heart of things.

And when my voice is silent in death, my song will speak in your living heart.

孩子天使

他们喧哗争斗，他们怀疑失望，他们辩论而没有结果。

我的孩子，让你的生命到他们当中去，如一线镇定而纯洁之光，使他们愉悦而沉默。

他们的贪心和妒忌是残忍的；他们的话，好像暗藏的刀，渴欲饮血。

我的孩子，去，去站在他们愤懑的心中，把你和善的眼光落在它们上面，好像那傍晚的宽宏大量的和平，覆盖着日间的骚扰一样。

我的孩子，让他们望着你的脸，因此能够知道一切事物的意义；让他们爱你，因此他们能够相爱。

来，坐在无垠的胸膛上，我的孩子。朝阳出来时，开放而且抬起你的心，像一朵盛开的花；夕阳落下时，低下你的头，默默地做完这一天的礼拜。

THE CHILD-ANGEL

THEY clamour and fight, they doubt and despair, they know no end to their wranglings.

Let your life come amongst them like a flame of light, my child, unflickering and pure, and delight them into silence.

They are cruel in their greed and their envy, their words are like hidden knives thirsting for blood.

Go and stand amidst their scowling hearts, my child, and let your gentle eyes fall upon them like the forgiving peace of the evening over the strife of the day.

Let them see your face, my child, and thus know the meaning of all things; let them love you and thus love each other.

Come and take your seat in the bosom of the limitless, my child. At sunrise open and raise your heart like a blossoming flower, and at sunset bend your head and in silence complete the worship of the day.

最后的买卖

早晨，我在石铺的路上走时，我叫道："谁来雇用我呀。"

皇帝坐着马车，手里拿着剑走来。

他拉着我的手，说道："我要用权力来雇用你。"

但是他的权力算不了什么，他坐着马车走了。

正午炎热的时候，家家户户的门都闭着。

我沿着屈曲的小巷走去。

一个老人带着一袋金钱走出来。

他斟酌了一下，说道："我要用金钱来雇用你。"

他一个一个地数着他的钱，但我却转身离去了。

黄昏了，花园的篱上满开着花。

美人走出来，说道：“我要用微笑来雇用你。”

她的微笑黯淡了，化成泪容了，她孤寂地回身走进黑暗里去。

太阳照耀在沙地上，海波任性地浪花四溅。

一个小孩坐在那里玩贝壳。

他抬起头来，好像认识我似的，说道：“我雇你不用什么东西。”

从此以后，在这个小孩的游戏中做成的买卖，使我成了一个自由的人。

THE LAST BARGAIN

"COME and hire me," I cried, while in the morning I was walking on the stone-paved road.

Sword in hand, the King came in his chariot.

He held my hand and said, "I will hire you with my power."

But his power counted for nought, and he went away in his chariot.

In the heat of the midday the houses stood with shut doors.

I wandered along the crooked lane.

An old man came out with his bag of gold.

He pondered and said, "I will hire you with my money."

He weighed his coins one by one, but I turned away.

It was evening. The garden hedge was all aflower.

The fair maid came out and said, "I will hire you with a smile."

Her smile paled and melted into tears, and she went back alone into the dark.

The sun glistened on the sand, and the sea waves broke waywardly.

A child sat playing with shells.

He raised his head and seemed to know me, and said, "I hire you with nothing."

From thenceforward that bargain struck in child' s play made me a free man.

飞鸟集

STRAY BIRDS

夏天的飞鸟，
飞到我的窗前唱歌，
又飞去了。
秋天的黄叶，
它们没有什么可唱，
只叹息一声，
飞落在那里。

Stray birds of summer come to my window to sing and fly away.

And yellow leaves of autumn, which have no songs, flutter and fall there with a sigh.

世界上的一队小小的漂泊者呀，
请留下你们的足印在我的文
字里。

O Troupe of little vagrants of the world, leave your footprints in my words.

世界对着它的爱人，
把它浩瀚的面具揭下了。
它变小了，
小如一首歌，
小如一回永恒的接吻。

The world puts off its mask of vastness to its lover.

It becomes small as one song, as one kiss of the eternal.

是大地的泪点，
使她的微笑保持着青春不谢。

It is the tears of the earth that keep her smiles in bloom.

无垠的沙漠热烈追求一叶绿草的爱，
她摇摇头笑着飞开了。

The mighty desert is burning for the love of a blade of grass who shakes her head and laughs and flies away.

如果你因失去了太阳而流泪，
那么你也将失去群星了。

If you shed tears when you miss the sun, you also miss the stars.

跳舞着的流水呀，
在你途中的泥沙，
要求你的歌声，
你的流动呢。你肯挟跛足的泥沙而俱下吗？

The sands in your way beg for your song and your movement, dancing water. Will you carry the burden of their lameness?

她热切的脸，
如夜雨似的，
搅扰着我的梦魂。

Her wishful face haunts my dreams like the rain at night.

有一次，
我们梦见大家都是不相识的。
我们醒了，
却知道我们原是相亲相爱的。

Once we dreamt that we were strangers.
We wake up to find that we were dear to each other.

忧思在我的心里平静下去，
正如暮色降临在寂静的山林中。

Sorrow is hushed into peace in my heart like the evening among the silent trees.

有些看不见的手指，
如懒懒的微风似的，
正在我的心上奏着潺湲的乐声。

Some unseen fingers, like an idle breeze, are playing upon my heart the music of the ripples.

“海水呀，
你说的是什么？”
“是永恒的疑问。”
“天空呀，
你回答的话是什么？”
“是永恒的沉默。”

What language is thine, O sea?

The language of eternal question.

What language is thy answer, O sky?

The language of eternal silence.

静静地听，
我的心呀，
听那世界的低语，
这是它对你求爱的表示呀。

Listen, my heart, to the whispers of the world with which it makes love to you.

创造的神秘，
有如夜间的黑暗——
是伟大的，而知识的幻影却不过
如晨间之雾。

The mystery of creation is like the darkness of night — it is great.

Delusions of knowledge are like the fog of the morning.

不要因为峭壁是高的，
便让你的爱情坐在峭壁上。

Do not seat your love upon a precipice because it is high.

我今晨坐在窗前，
世界如一个路人似的，
停留了一会，
向我点点头又走过去了。

I sit at my window this morning where the world like a passer-by stops for a moment, nods to me and goes.

这些微风，
是树叶的簌簌之声呀；它们在我的心里欢悦地微语着。

There little thoughts are the rustle of leaves; they have their whisper of joy in my mind.

你看不见你自己，
你所看见的只是你的影子。

What you are you do not see, what you see is your shadow.

神呀，
我的那些愿望真是愚蠢呀，
它们杂在你的歌声中喧叫着呢。
让我只是静听着吧。

My wishes are fools, they shout across thy song, my Master. Let me but listen.

我不能选择那最好的。
是那最好的选择我。

I cannot choose the best. The best chooses me.

那些把灯背在背上的人，
把他们的影子投到了自己前面。

They throw their shadows before them who carry their lantern on their back.

我的存在，
对我是一个永久的神奇，
这就是生活。

That I exist is a perpetual surprise which is life.

“我们萧萧的树叶都有声响回答那风和雨。你是谁呢，
那样地沉默着？”
“我不过是一朵花。”

We, the rustling leaves, have a voice that answers the storms, but who are you so silent?
I am a mere flower.

休息与工作的关系，
正如眼睑与眼睛的关系。

Rest belongs to the work as the eyelids to the eyes.

人是一个初生的孩子，
他的力量，
就是生长的力量。

Man is a born child, his power is the power of growth.

神希望我们酬答他，
在于他送给我们的花朵，
而不在于太阳和土地。

God expects answers for the flowers he sends us, not for the sun, the earth.

光明如一个裸体的孩子，
快活地在绿叶当中游戏，
它不知道人是会欺诈的。

The light that plays, like a naked child, among the green leaves happily knows not that man can lie.

啊，
美呀，
在爱中找你自己吧，
不要到你镜子的谄谀去找寻。

O Beauty, find thyself in love, not in the flattery of thy mirror.

我的心把她的波浪在世界的海岸上冲激着，
以热泪在上边写着她的题记：
"我爱你。"

My heart beats her waves at the shore of the world and writes upon it her signature in tears with the words, I love thee.

“月儿呀，
你在等候什么呢？”
“向我将让位给他的太阳致敬。”

*Moon, for what do you wait?
To salute the sun for
whom I must make way.*

绿树长到了我的窗前，
仿佛是喑哑的大地发出的渴望的
声音。

*The trees come up to my
window like the yearning
voice of the dumb earth.*

神自己的清晨，
在他自己看来也是新奇的。

His own mornings are new surprises to God.

生命从世界得到资产，
爱情使它得到价值。

Life finds its wealth by the claims of the world, and its worth by the claims of love.

枯竭的河床，
并不感谢它的过去。

The dry river-bed finds no thanks for its past.

鸟儿愿为一朵云。
云儿愿为一只鸟。

The bird wishes it were a cloud.The cloud wishes it were a bird.

枯竭的河床，
并不感谢它的过去。

The dry river-bed finds no thanks for its past.

鸟儿愿为一朵云。
云儿愿为一只鸟。

The bird wishes it were a cloud.
The cloud wishes it were a bird.

瀑布歌唱道：“我得到自由时便有了歌声了。”

The waterfall sing, “I find my song, when I find my freedom.”

我说不出这心为什么那样默默地颓丧着。
是为了它那不曾要求，
不曾知道，
不曾记得的小小的需要。

I cannot tell why this heart languishes in silence.
It is for small needs it never asks, or knows or remembers.

妇人，
你在料理家务的时候，
你的手足歌唱着，
正如山间的溪水歌唱着，
在小石中流过。

Woman, when you move about in your household service your limbs sing like a hill stream among its pebbles.

当太阳横过西方的海面时，
对着东方留下他最后的敬礼。

The sun goes to cross the Western sea, leaving its last salutation to the East.

不要因为你自己没有胃口，而去责备你的食物。

Do not blame your food because you have no appetite.

群树如表示大地的愿望似的，踮起脚来向天空窥望。

The trees, like the longings of the earth, stand atiptoe to peep at the heaven.

你微微地笑着，
不同我说什么话。而我觉得，
为了这个，
我已经等待很久。

You smiled and talked to me of nothing and I felt that for this I had been waiting long.

水里的游鱼是沉默的，
陆地上的兽类是喧闹的，
空中的飞鸟是歌唱着的。
但是，
人类却兼有海里的沉默，
地上的喧闹与空中的音乐。

The fish in the water is silent, the animal on the earth is noisy, the bird in the air is singing.

But Man has in him the silence of the sea, the noise of the earth and the music of the air.

世界在踌躇之心的琴弦上跑
过去，
奏出忧郁的乐声。

The world rushes on over the strings of the lingering heart making the music of sadness.

他把他的刀剑当作他的上帝。
当他的刀剑胜利的时候，
他自己却失败了。

He has made his weapons his gods.

When his weapons win he is defeated himself.

神从创造中找到他自己。

God finds himself by creating.

“阴影”戴上她的面幕，
秘密地、温顺地，
用她沉默的爱的脚步，
跟在“光”的后面。

Shadow, with her veil drawn, follows Light in secret meekness, with her silent steps of love.

群星不怕显得像萤火那样。

The stars are not afraid to appear like fireflies.

谢谢神，
我不是一个权力的轮子，
而是被压在这轮子下的活人
之一。

I thank thee that I am none of the wheels of power but I am one with the living creatures that are crushed by it.

心是尖锐的，
不是宽博的，
它执着在每一点上，
却并不活动。

The mind, sharp but not broad, sticks at every point but does not move.

你的偶像委散在尘土中了，
这可证明神的尘土比你的偶像还
伟大。

Your idol is shattered in the dust to prove that God's dust is greater than your idol.

人不能在他的历史中表现出他
自己，
他在历史中奋斗着露出头角。

Man does not reveal himself in his history, he struggles up through it.

玻璃灯因为瓦灯叫它做表兄而责
备瓦灯。但明月出来时，
玻璃灯却温和地微笑着，
叫明月为——“我亲爱的，
亲爱的姊姊。”

While the glass lamp rebukes the earthen for calling it cousin, the moon rises, and the glass lamp, with a bland smile, calls her, — My dear, dear sister.

我们如海鸥之与波涛相遇似的，
遇见了，
走近了。海鸥飞去，
波涛滚滚地流开，
我们也分别了。

Like the meeting of the seagulls and the waves we meet and come near. The seagulls fly off, the waves roll away and we depart.

我的白昼已经完了，
我像一只泊在海滩上的小船，
谛听着晚潮跳舞的乐声。

My day is done, and I am like a boat drawn on the beach, listening to the dance-music of the tide in the evening.

我们的生命是天赋的，
我们惟有献出生命，
才能得到生命。

Life is given to us, we earn it by giving it.

当我们是大为谦卑的时候，
便是我们最接近伟大的时候。

We come nearest to the great when we are great in humility.

麻雀看见孔雀负担着它的翎尾，
替它担忧。

The sparrow is sorry for the peacock at the burden of its tail.

决不要害怕刹那——永恒之声这样唱着。

Never be afraid of the moments — thus sings the voice of the everlasting.

风于无路之中寻求最短之路，
又突然地在“无何有之国”终止
了它的追求。

The hurricane seeks the shortest road by the no-road, and suddenly ends its search in the Nowhere.

在我自己的杯中，
饮了我的酒吧，朋友。
一倒在别人的杯里，
这酒里腾跳的泡沫便要消失了。

Take my wine in my own cup, friend.
It loses its wreath of foam when poured into that of others.

“完全”为了对“不全”的爱，
把自己装饰得美丽。

The perfect decks itself in beauty for the love of the Imperfect.

神对人说：“我医治你，
所以伤害你；爱你，所以惩
罚你。”

God says to man, "I heal you therefore I hurt, love you therefore punish."

谢谢火焰给你光明，
但是不要忘了那执灯的人，
他是坚忍地站在黑暗当中呢。

Thank the flame for its light, but do not forget the lampholder standing in the shade with constancy of patience.

小草呀，
你的步履虽小，
但是你拥有你足下的土地。

Tiny grass, your steps are small, but you possess the earth under your tread.

幼花的蓓蕾开放了，
它叫道："亲爱的世界呀，
请不要萎谢了。"

The infant flower opens its bud and cries, "Dear World, please do not fade."

神对于那些大帝国会感到厌恶，
却决不会厌恶那些小小的花朵。

God grows weary of great kingdoms, but never of little flowers.

错误经不起失败，
但是真理却不怕失败。

Wrong cannot afford defeat but Right can.

瀑布歌唱道："虽然渴者只要少
许的水便够了，
我却很快活地给与了我全部
的水。"

"I give my whole water in joy," sings the waterfall, "though it is enough for the thirsty."

把那些花朵抛掷上去的那一阵子
无休无止、狂欢大喜的劲儿，
其源泉是在哪里呢？

Where is the fountain that throws up these flowers in a ceaseless outbreak of ecstasy?

樵夫的斧头，
问树要斧柄。
树便给了他。

The woodcutter's axe begged for its handle from the tree. The tree gave it.

这寡独的黄昏，
幕着雾与雨，
我在我心的孤寂里，
感觉到它的叹息。

In my solitude of heart I feel the sigh of this widowed evening veiled with mist and rain.

贞操是从丰富的爱情中生出来的财富。

Chastity is a wealth that comes from abundance of love.

雾，
像爱情一样，
在山峰的心上游戏，
生出种种美丽的变幻。

The mist, like love, plays upon the heart of the hills and bring out surprises of beauty.

我们把世界看错了，
反说它欺骗我们。

We read the world wrong and say that it deceives us.

诗人——飙风，
正出经海洋森林，
追求它自己的歌声。

The poet wind is out over the sea and the forest to seek his own voice.

每一个孩子出生时，
都带来信息说：神对人并未灰心失望。

Every child comes with the message that God is not yet discouraged of man.

绿草求她地上的伴侣。
树木求他天空的寂寞。

The grass seeks her crowd in the earth.
The tree seeks his solitude of the sky.

人对他自己建筑起堤防来。

Man barricades against himself.

我的朋友，
你的语声飘荡在我的心里，
像那海水的低吟声绕缭在静听着
的松林之间。

Your voice, my friend, wanders in my heart, like the muffled sound of the sea among these listening pines.

这个不可见的黑暗之火焰，
以繁星为其火花，
到底是什么呢？

What is this unseen flame of darkness whose sparks are the stars?

使生如夏花之绚烂，
死如秋叶之静美。

Let life be beautiful like summer flowers and death like autumn leaves.

那想做好人的，
在门外敲着门；那爱人的，
看见门敞开着。

He who wants to do good knocks at the gate; he who loves finds the gate open.

在死的时候，
众多合而为一；在生的时候，
一化为众多。
神死了的时候，
宗教便将合而为一。

In death the many becomes one; in life the one becomes many.
Religion will be one when God is dead.

艺术家是自然的情人，
所以他是自然的奴隶，
也是自然的主人。

The artist is the lover of Nature, therefore he is her slave and her master.

“你离我有多远呢，
果实呀？”
“我藏在你心里呢，
花呀。”

How far are you from me, O Fruit?
I am hidden in your heart, O Flower.

这个渴望是为了那个在黑夜里感觉得到，在大白天里却看不见的人。

This longing is for the one who is felt in the dark, but not seen in the day.

露珠对湖水说道："你是在荷叶下面的大露珠，我是在荷叶上面较小的露珠。"

"You are the big drop of dew under the lotus leaf, I am the smaller one on its upper side," said the dewdrop to the lake.

刀鞘保护刀的锋利，
它自己则满足于它的迟钝。

The scabbard is content to be dull when it protects the keenness of the sword.

在黑暗中，
“一”视如一体；在光亮中，
“一”便视如众多。

In darkness the One appears as uniform; in the light the One appears as manifold.

大地借助于绿草，
显出她自己的殷勤好客。

The great earth makes herself hospitable with the help of the grass.

绿叶的生与死乃是旋风急骤的旋转，
它更广大的旋转的圈子乃是在天上繁星之间徐缓地转动。

The birth and death of the leaves are the rapid whirls of the eddy whose wider circles move slowly among stars.

权势对世界说道：“你我的。”
世界便把权势囚禁在她的宝座下面。
爱情对世界说道：“我是你的。”
世界便给予爱情以在她屋内来往的自由。

Power said to the world, "You are mine."

The world kept it prisoner on her throne.

Love said to the world, "I am thine."

The world gave it the freedom of her house.

浓雾仿佛是大地的愿望。
它藏起了太阳，
而太阳原是它所呼求的。

The mist is like the earth' s desire.

It hides the sun for whom she cries.

安静些吧，
我的心，
这些大树都是祈祷者呀。

Be still, my heart, these great trees are prayers.

瞬刻的喧声讥笑着永恒的音乐。

The noise of the moment scoffs at the music of the Eternal.

我想起了浮泛在生与爱与死的川流上许多别的时代，
以及这些时代之被遗忘，
我便感觉到离开尘世的自由了。

I think of other ages that floated upon the stream of life and love and death and are forgotten, and I feel the freedom of passing away.

我灵魂里的忧郁就是她新婚的面纱，这面纱等候着在夜间卸去。

The sadness of my soul is her bride's veil.
It waits to be lifted in the night.

死之印记给生的钱币以价值，
使它能够用生命来购买那真正的宝物。

Death's stamp gives value to the coin of life; making it possible to buy with life what is truly precious.

白云谦逊地站在天之一隅。
晨光给它戴上霞彩。

The cloud stood humbly in a corner of the sky.
The morning crowned it with splendour.

尘土受到损辱，
却以她的花朵来报答。

The dust receives insult and in return offers her flowers.

只管走过去，
不必逗留着采了花朵来保存，
因为一路上花朵自会继续开
放的。

Do not linger to gather flowers to keep them, but walk on, for flowers will keep themselves blooming all your way.

根是地下的枝。
枝是空中的根。

Roots are the branches down in the earth.
Branches are roots in the air.

远远去了的夏之音乐，
翱翔于秋间，
寻求它的旧垒。

The music of the far-away summer flutters around the Autumn seeking its former nest.

不要从你自己的袋里掏出勋绩借给你的朋友，
这是污辱他。

Do not insult your friend by lending him merits from your own pocket.

无名日子的感触，
攀缘在我的心上，
正像那绿色的苔藓，
攀缘在老树的周身。

The touch of the nameless days clings to my heart like mosses round the old tree.

回声嘲笑它的原声，
以证明它是原声。

The echo mocks her origin to prove she is the original.

当富贵利达的人夸说他得到神的
特别恩惠时，上帝却羞了。

God is ashamed when the prosperous boasts of His special favour.

我投射我自己的影子在我的
路上，
因为我有一盏还没有燃点起来的
明灯。

I cast my own shadow upon my path, because I have a lamp that has not been lighted.

人走进喧哗的群众里去，
为的是要淹没他自己沉默的
呼号。

Man goes into the noisy crowd to drown his own clamour of silence.

终止于衰竭是“死亡”，
但“圆满”却终止于无穷。

That which ends in exhaustion is death, but the perfect ending is in the endless.

太阳只穿一件朴素的光衣，
白云却披了灿烂的裙裾。

The sun has his simple robe of light. The clouds are decked with gorgeousness.

山峰如群儿之喧嚷，
举起它们的双臂，
想去捉天上的星星。

The hills are like shouts of children who raise their arms, trying to catch stars.

道路虽然拥挤，
却是寂寞的，
因为它是不被爱的。

The road is lonely in its crowd for it is not loved.

权势以它的恶行自夸，
落下的黄叶与浮游的云片却在笑它。

The power that boasts of its mischiefs is laughed at by the yellow leaves that fall, and clouds that pass by.

今天，
大地在太阳光里向我营营哼鸣，
像一个织着布的妇人，
用一种已经被忘却的语言，
哼着一些古代的歌曲。

The earth hums to me today in the sun, like a woman at her spinning, some ballad of the ancient time in a forgotten tongue.

绿草是无愧于它所生长的伟大世界的。

The grass-blade is worthy of the great world where it grows.

梦是一个一定要谈话的妻子。
睡眠是一个默默忍受的丈夫。

Dream is a wife who must talk,
Sleep is a husband who silently suffers.

夜与逝去的日子接吻，
轻轻地在他耳旁说道：“我是死，
是你的母亲。我就要给你以新的生命。

The night kisses the fading day whispering to his ear, "I am death, your mother. I am to give you fresh birth."

黑夜呀，
我感觉到你的美了。你的美如一个可爱的妇人，
当她把灯灭了的时候。

I feel thy beauty, dark night, like that of the loved woman when she has put out the lamp.

我把那些已逝去的世界上的繁荣带到我的世界上来。

I carry in my world that flourishes the worlds that have failed.

亲爱的朋友呀，
当我静听着海涛时，
我好几次在暮色深沉的黄昏里，
在这个海岸上，
感到你伟大思想的沉默了。

Dear friend, I feel the silence of your great thoughts of many a deepening eventide on this beach when I listen to these waves.

鸟以为把鱼举在空中是一种慈善的举动。

The bird thinks it is an act of kindness to give the fish a life in the air.

夜对太阳说道："在月亮中，你送了你的情书给我。"
"我已在绿草上留下了我流着泪点的回答了。"

"In the moon thou sendest thy love letters to me,"said the night to the sun.

"I leave my answers in tears upon the grass."

伟人是一个天生的孩子，
当他死时，
他把他伟大的孩提时代给了世界。

The great is a born child; when he dies he gives his great childhood to the world.

不是槌的打击，
乃是水的载歌载舞，
使鹅卵石臻于完美。

Not hammer-strokes, but dance of the water sings the pebbles into perfection.

蜜蜂从花中啜蜜，
离开时嘤嘤地道谢。
浮华的蝴蝶却相信花是应该向它道谢的。

Bees sip honey from flowers and hum their thanks when they leave.

The gaudy butterfly is sure that the flowers owe thanks to him.

如果你不等待着要说出完全的真理，
那么把真话说出来是很容易的。

To be outspoken is easy when you do not wait to speak the complete truth.

“可能”问“不可能”道：
“你住在什么地方呢？”
它回答道：“在那无能为力者的梦境里。”

Asks the Possible to the Impossible,
Where is your dwelling-place?
In the dreams of the impotent, comes the answer.

如果你把所有的错误都关在门外时，
真理也要被关在门外面了。

If you shut your door to all errors truth will be shut out.

我听见有些东西在我心的忧闷后面萧萧作响——我不能看见它们。

I hear some rustle of things behind my sadness of heart,
— I cannot see them.

闲暇在动作时便是工作。
静止的海水荡动时便成波涛。

Leisure in its activity is work.
The stillness of the sea stirs in waves.

绿叶恋爱时，
便成了花。
花崇拜时，
便成了果实。

The leaf becomes flower when it loves.
The flower becomes fruit when it worships.

埋在地下的树根使树枝产生果实，
却不要什么报酬。

The roots below the earth claim no rewards for making the branches fruitful.

阴雨的黄昏，
风无休止地吹着。
我看着摇曳的树枝，
想念万物的伟大。

This rainy evening the wind is restless.

I look at the swaying branches and ponder over the greatness of all things.

子夜的风雨，
如一个巨大的孩子，
在不合时宜的黑夜里醒来，
开始游戏和喧闹。

Storm of midnight, like a giant child awakened in the untimely dark, has begun to play and shout.

海呀，
你这暴风雨的孤寂的新妇呀，
你虽掀起波浪追随你的情人，
但是无用呀。

Thou raisest thy waves vainly to follow thy lover, O sea, thou lonely bride of the storm.

文字对工作说道：“我惭愧我的空虚。”
工作对文字说道：“当我看见你时，我便知道我是怎样的贫乏了。”

"I am ashamed of my emptiness," said the Word to the Work.

"I know how poor I am when I see you," said the Work to the Word.

时间是变化的财富。时钟模仿它，
却只有变化而无财富。

Time is the wealth of change,
but the clock in its parody
makes it mere change and no
wealth.

真理穿了衣裳，
觉得事实太拘束了。
在想象中，
她却转动得很舒畅。

Truth in her dress finds facts
too tight.
In fiction she moves with ease.

当我到这里那里旅行着时，
路呀，
我厌倦你了；但是现在，
当你引导我到各处去时我便爱上
你，与你结婚了。

When I travelled to here and to there, I was tired of thee, O Road, but now when thou leadest me to everywhere I am wedded to thee in love.

让我设想，
在群星之中，
有一颗星是指导着我的生命通过
不可知的黑暗的。

Let me think that there is one among those stars that guides my life through the dark unknown.

妇人，
你用了你美丽的手指，
触着我的什物，
秩序便如音乐似的生出来了。

Woman, with the grace of your fingers you touched my things and order came out like music.

一个忧郁的声音，
筑巢于逝水似的年华中。
它在夜里向我唱道：“我
爱你。”

One sad voice has its nest among the ruins of the years.

It sings to me in the night, —I loved you.

燃着的火，
以它熊熊的光焰，
警告我不要走近它。
把我从潜藏在灰中的余烬里救出
来吧。

The flaming fire warns me off by its own glow.

Save me from the dying embers hidden under ashes.

我有群星在天上，
但是，
唉，
我屋里的小灯却没有点亮。

I have my stars in the sky.

But oh for my little lamp unlit in my house.

死文字的尘土沾着你。
用沉默去洗净你的灵魂吧。

The dust of the dead words clings to thee.
Wash thy soul with silence.

生命里留了许多罅隙，
从中送来了死之忧郁的音乐。

Gaps are left in life through which comes the sad music of death.

世界已在早晨敞开了它的光明之心。
出来吧，我的心，
带着你的爱去与它相会。

The world has opened its heart of light in the morning.

Come out, my heart, with thy love to meet it.

我的思想随着这些闪耀的绿叶而闪耀；我的心灵因为这日光的抚触而歌唱；我的生命因为偕了万物一同浮泛在空间的蔚蓝、时间的墨黑而感到欢快。

My thoughts shimmer with these shimmering leaves and my heart sings with the touch of this sunlight; my life is glad to be floating with all things into the blue of space, into the dark of time.

神巨大的威权是在柔和的微风里，而不在狂风暴雨之中。

God's great power is in the gentle breeze, not in the storm.

在梦中，
一切事都散漫着，都压着我，
但这不过是一个梦呀。但我醒来时，
我便将觉得这些事都已聚集在你那里，我也便将自由了。

This is a dream in which things are all loose and they oppress.

I shall find them gathered in thee when I awake and shall be free.

落日问道："有谁继续我的职务呢？"
瓦灯说道："我要尽我所能地做去，我的主人。"

"Who is there to take up my duties?" asked the setting sun.
"I shall do what I can, my Master," said the earthen lamp.

采着花瓣时，
得不到花的美丽。

By plucking her petals you do not gather the beauty of the flower.

沉默蕴蓄着语声，
正如鸟巢拥围着睡鸟。

Silence will carry your voice like the nest that holds the sleeping birds.

大的不怕与小的同游。
居中的却远而避之。

The Greatv walks with the Small without fear.
The Middling keeps aloof.

夜秘密地把花开放了，
却让白日去领受谢词。

The night opens the flowers in secret and allows the day to get thanks.

权势认为牺牲者的痛苦是忘恩负义。

Power takes as ingratitude the writhings of its victims.

当我们以我们的充实为乐时，
那么，我们便能很快乐地跟我们
的果实分手了。

When we rejoice in our fulness, then we can part with our fruits with joy.

雨点吻着大地，
微语道："我们是你思家的孩子，
母亲，现在从天上回到你这里
来了。"

The raindrops kissed the earth and whispered, — We are thy homesick children, mother, come back to thee from the heaven.

蛛网好像要捉露珠，
却捉住了苍蝇。

The cobweb pretends to catch dewdrops and catches flies.

爱情呀，
当你手里拿着点亮了的痛苦之灯
走来时，
我能够看见你的脸，
而且以你为幸福。

Love! When you come with the burning lamp of pain in your hand, I can see your face and know you as bliss.

萤火对天上的星说道：“学者说你的光明总有一天会消灭的。”
天上的星不回答它。

"The leaned say that your lights will one day be no more," said the firefly to the stars.
The stars made no answer.

在黄昏的微光里，
有那清晨的鸟儿来到了我沉默的鸟巢里。

In the dusk of the evening the bird of some early dawn comes to the nest of my silence.

思想掠过我的心上，
如一群野鸭飞过天空。
我听见它们鼓翼之声了。

Thoughts pass in my mind like flocks of ducks in the sky. I hear the voice of their wings.

沟洫总喜欢想：河流的存在，
是专为它供给水流的。

The canal loves to think that rivers exist solely to supply it with water.

世界以它的痛苦同我接吻，
而要求歌声做报酬。

The world has kissed my soul with its pain, asking for its return in songs.

压迫着我的，
到底是我想要外出的灵魂呢，
还是那世界的灵魂，敲着我的
心门，
想要进来呢？

That which oppresses me, is it my soul trying to come out in the open, or the soul of the world knocking at my heart for its entrance?

思想以他自己的语言喂养它自己，
而成长起来了。

Thought feeds itself with its own words and grows.

我把我心之碗轻轻浸入这沉默之时刻中，它盛满了爱。

I have dipped the vessel of my heart into this silent hour; it has filled with love.

或者你在工作，
或者你没有。
当你不得不说：“让我们做些事吧”时，
那么就要开始胡闹了。

Either you have work or you have not.

When you have to say, "Let us do something", then begins mischief.

向日葵羞于把无名的花朵看作它的同胞。

太阳升上来了，向它微笑，说道："你好吗，我的宝贝儿？"

The sunflower blushed to own the nameless flower as her kin.

The sun rose and smiled on it, saying, "Are you well, my darling?"

"谁如命运似的催着我向前走呢？"

"那是我自己，在身背后大跨步走着。"

Who drives me forward like fate?

The Myself striding on my back.

云把水倒在河的水杯里，
它们自己却藏在远山之中。

The clouds fill the watercups of the river, hiding themselves in the distant hills.

我一路走去，
从我的水瓶中漏出水来。
只剩下极少极少的水供我回家使用。

I spill water from my water jar as I walk on my way,

Very little remains for my home.

杯中的水是光辉的，
海中的水却是黑色的。
小理可以用文字来说清楚，
大理却只有沉默。

The water in a vessel is sparkling; the water in the sea is dark.

The small truth has words that are clear; the great truth has great silence.

你的微笑是你自己田园里的花，
你的谈吐是你自己山上松林的萧萧；但是你的心呀，
却是那个女人，
那个我们全都认识的女人。

Your smile was the flowers of your own fields, your talk was the rustle of your own mountain pines, but your heart was the woman that we all know.

我把小小的礼物留给我所爱的人——大的礼物却留给一切的人。

It is the little things that I leave behind for my loved ones, — great things are for everyone.

妇人呀，
你用泪海包绕着世界的心，
正如大海包绕着大地。

Woman, thou hast encircled the world' s heart with the depth of thy tears as the sea has the earth.

太阳以微笑向我问候。
雨，
他忧郁的姊姊，
向我的心谈话。

The sunshine greets me with a smile.

The rain, his sad sister, talks to my heart.

我的昼间之花，
落下它那被遗忘的花瓣。
在黄昏中，
这花成熟为一颗记忆的金果。

My flower of the day dropped its petals forgotten.

In the evening it ripens into a golden fruit of memory.

我像那夜间之路，
正静悄悄地谛听着记忆的足音。

I am like the road in the night listening to the footfalls of its memories in silence.

黄昏的天空，
在我看来，
像一扇窗户，
一盏灯火，
灯火背后的一次等待。

The evening sky to me is like a window, and a lighted lamp, and a waiting behind it.

太急于做好事的人，
反而找不到时间去做好人。

He who is too busy doing good finds no time to be good.

我是秋云，
空空地不载着雨水，
但在成熟的稻田中，
可以看见我的充实。

I am the autumn cloud, empty of rain, see my fulness in the field of ripened rice.

他们嫉妒，
他们残杀，
人反而称赞他们。
然而上帝却害了羞，
匆匆地把他的记忆埋藏在绿草
下面。

They hated and killed and men praised them.

But God in shame hastens to hide its memory under the green grass.

脚趾乃是舍弃了其过去的手指。

Toes are the fingers that have forsaken their past.

黑暗向光明旅行，
但是盲者却向死亡旅行。

Darkness travels towards light, but blindness towards death.

小狗疑心大宇宙阴谋篡夺它的位置。

The pet dog suspects the universe for scheming to take its place.

静静地坐着吧，
我的心，
不要扬起你的尘土。
让世界自己寻路向你走来。

Sit still, my heart, do not raise your dust.
Let the world find its way to you.

弓在箭要射出之前，
低声对箭说道："你的自由就是我的自由。"

The bow whispers to the arrow before it speeds forth — Your freedom is mine.

妇人，
在你的笑声里有着生命之泉的音乐。

Woman, in your laughter you have the music of the fountain of life.

全是理智的心，
恰如一柄全是锋刃的刀。
它叫使用它的人手上流血。

A mind all logic is like a knife all blade.
It makes the hand bleed that uses it.

神爱人间的灯光甚于他自己的大星。

God loves man' s lamp lights better than his own great stars.

这世界乃是为美之音乐所驯服了的狂风骤雨的世界。

This world is the world of wild storms kept tame with the music of beauty.

晚霞向太阳说道："我的心经了你的接吻，
便似金的宝箱了。"

"My heart is like the golden casket of thy kiss," said the sunset cloud to the sun.

接触着，
你许会杀害；远离着，
你许会占有。

By touching you may kill, by keeping away you may possess.

蟋蟀的唧唧，
夜雨的淅沥，
从黑暗中传到我的耳边，
好似我已逝的少年时代，
沙沙地来到我的梦境中。

The cricket's chirp and the patter of rain come to me through the dark, like the rustle of dreams from my past youth.

花朵向星辰落尽了的曙天叫道：
“我的露珠全失落了。”

"I have lost my dewdrop," cried the flower to the morning sky that has lost all its stars.

燃烧着的木块，
熊熊地生出火光，
叫道："这是我的花朵，
我的死亡。"

The burning log bursts in flame and cries, — "This is my flower, my death."

黄蜂认为邻蜂储蜜之巢太小。
它的邻人要它去建筑一个更
小的。

The wasp thinks that the honeyhive of the neighbouring bees is too small.
His neighbours ask him to build one still smaller.

河岸向河流说道："我不能留住
你的波浪。
让我保存你的足印在我的心
里吧。"

"I cannot keep your waves," says the bank to tle river.
"Let me keep your footprints in my heart."

白日以这小小的地球的喧扰，
淹没了整个宇宙的沉默。

The day, with the noise of this little earth, drowns the silence of all worlds.

歌声在天空中感到无限，
图画在地上感到无限，
诗呢，无论在空中，
在地上都是如此。因为诗的词句
含有能走动的意义与能飞翔的
音乐。

The song feels the infinite in the air, the picture in the earth, the poem in the air and the earth; For its words have meaning that walks and music that soars.

太阳在西方落下时，
它的早晨的东方已静悄悄地站在
它面前。

When the sun goes down to the West, the East of his morning stands before him in silence.

让我不要错误地把自己放在我的
世界里，
而使它反对我。

Let me not put myself wrongly to my world and set it against me.

荣誉使我感到惭愧，
因为我暗地里求着它。

Praise shames me, for I secretly beg for it.

当我没有什么事做时，
便让我不做什么事，
不受骚扰地沉入安静深处吧，
一如那海水沉默时海边的暮色。

Let my doing nothing when I have nothing to do become untroubled in its depth of peace like the evening in the seashore when the water is silent.

少女呀，
你的淳朴，
如湖水之碧，
表现出你的真理之深邃。

Maiden, your simplicity, like the blueness of the lake, reveals your depth of truth.

最好的东西不是独来的，
它伴了所有的东西同来。

The best does not come alone. It comes with the company of the all.

神的右手是慈爱的，
但是他的左手却可怕。

God's right hand is gentle, but terrible is his left hand.

我的晚色从陌生的树木中走来，
它用我的晓星所不懂得的语言
说话。

My evening came among the alien trees and spoke in a language which my morning stars did not know.

夜之黑暗是一只口袋，
迸出黎明的金光。

Night's darkness is a bag that bursts with the gold of the dawn.

我们的欲望把彩虹的颜色借给那
只不过是云雾的人生。

Our desire lends the colours of the rainbow to the mere mists and vapours of life.

神等待着，
要从人的手上，
把他自己的花朵作为礼物赢得
回去。

God waits to win back his own flowers as gifts from man's hands.

我的忧思缠绕着我，
要问我，
它自己的名字。

My sad thoughts tease me asking me their own names.

果的事业是尊贵的，
花的事业是甜美的；但是让我做
叶的事业吧，
叶是谦逊的，
专心地垂着绿荫的。

The service of the fruit is precious, the service of the flower is sweet, but let my service be the service of the leaves in its shade of humble devotion.

我的心向着阑珊的风张了帆，
要到无论何处的荫凉之岛去。

My heart has spread its sails to the idle winds for the shadowy island of Anywhere.

独夫们是凶暴的，
但人民是善良的。

Men are cruel, but Man is kind.

把我当作你的杯吧，
为了你，
为了你的人而盛满了水吧。

Make me thy cup and let my fulness be for thee and for thine.

狂风暴雨像是在痛苦中，
某个天神的哭声，
因为他的爱情被大地所拒绝。

The storm is like the cry of some god in pain whose love the earth refuses.

世界不会流失，
因为死亡并不是一个罅隙。

The world does not leak because death is not a crack.

生命因为付出了的爱情而更为富足。

Life has become richer by the love that has been lost.

我的朋友，
你伟大的心闪射出东方朝阳的光芒，
正如黎明中一个积雪的孤峰。

My friend, your great heart shone with the sunrise of the East like the snowy summit of a lonely hill in the dawn.

死之流泉，
使生的止水跳跃。

The fountain of death makes the still water of life play.

那些有一切东西而没有您的人，
我的上帝，
在讥笑着那些没有别的东西，
而只有您的人呢。

Those who have everything but thee, my God, laugh at those who have nothing but thyself.

生命的运动在它自己的音乐里，
得到它的休息。

The movement of life has its rest in its own music.

踢足只能从地上扬起尘土，
而不能得到收获。

Kicks only raise dust and not crops from the earth.

我们的名字，
便是夜里海波上发出的光，
痕迹也不留地就泯灭了。

Our names are the light that glows on the sea waves at night and then dies without leaving its signature.

让睁眼看着玫瑰花的人也看看它的刺。

Let him only see the thorns who has eyes to see the rose.

鸟翼上系上了黄金，
这鸟便永不能再在天上翱翔。

Set the bird's wings with gold and it will never again soar in the sky.

我们地方的荷花又在这陌生的水
上开了花，
放出同样的清香，
只是名字换了。

*The same lotus of our clime
blooms here in the alien
water with the same sweetness,
under another name.*

在心的远景里，
那相隔的距离显得更广阔了。

In heart's perspective the distance looms large.

月儿把她的光明遍照在天上，
却留着她的黑斑给她自己。

The moon has her light all over the sky, her dark spots to herself.

不要说：“这是早晨”，
别用一个“昨天”的名词把它打发掉。
你第一次看到它，
把它当作还没有名字的新生孩子吧。

Do not say, "It is morning," and dismiss it with a mane of yesterday.
See it for the first time as a new-born child that has no name.

青烟对天空夸口，
灰烬对大地夸口，
都以为它们是火的兄弟。

Smoke boasts to the sky, and Ashes to the earth, that they are brothers to the fire.

雨点向茉莉花微语道：“把我永久地留在你的心里吧。”
茉莉花叹息了一声，
落在地上了。

The raindrop whispered to the jasmine, "Keep me in your heart for ever."
The jasmine sighed, "Alas," and dropped to the ground.

胆怯的思想呀，
不要怕我。
我是一个诗人。

Timid thoughts, do not be afraid of me.
I am a poet.

我的心在朦胧的沉默里，
似乎充满了蟋蟀的鸣声——声音的灰暗的暮色。

The dim silence of my mind seems filled with crickets' chirp — the grey twilight of sound.

爆竹呀，
你对群星的侮蔑，
又跟着你自己回到地上来了。

Rockets, your insult to the stars follows yourself back to the earth.

您曾经带领着我，
穿过我白天拥挤不堪的旅程，
而到达了我黄昏孤寂之境。
在通宵的寂静里，
我等待着它的意义。

Thou hast led me through my crowded travels of the day to my evening' s loneliness.

I wait for its meaning through the stillness of the night.

我们的生命就似渡过一个大海，
我们都相聚在这个狭小的舟中。
死时，
我们便到了岸，
各往各的世界去了。

This life is the crossing of a sea, where we meet in the same narrow ship.

In death we reach the shore and go to our different worlds.

真理之川从它的错误之沟渠中流过。

The stream of truth flows through its channels of mistakes.

今天我的心是在想家了，
在想着那跨过时间之海的那一个
甜蜜的时候。

My heart is homesick today for the one sweet hour across the sea of time.

鸟的歌声是曙光从大地反响过去
的回声。

The bird-song is the echo of the morning light back from the earth.

晨光问毛茛道："你是骄傲得不肯和我接吻吗？"

"Are you too proud to kiss me?" the morning light asked the buttercup.

小花问道："我要怎样地对你唱，怎样地崇拜你呢，太阳呀？"
太阳答道："只要用你纯洁的素朴的沉默。"

"How may I sing to thee and worship, O Sun?" asked the little flower.

"By the simple silence of thy purity," answered the sun.

当人是兽时，
他比兽还坏。

Man is worse than an animal when he is an animal.

黑云受光的接吻时，
便变成天上的花朵。

Dark clouds become heaven's flowers when kissed by light.

不要让刀锋讥笑它柄子的拙钝。

Let not the sword-blade mock its handle for being blunt.

夜的沉默，
如一个深深的灯盏，
银河便是它燃着的灯光。

The night's silence, like a deep lamp, is burning with the light of its milky way.

死像大海无限的歌声，
日夜冲击着生命光明岛的四周。

Around the sunny island of Life swells day and night death' s limitless song of the sea.

花瓣似的山峰在饮着日光，
这山岂不像一朵花吗？

Is not this mountain like a flower, with its petals of hill, drinking the sunlight?

“真实”的含义被误解，
轻重被倒置，
那就成了“不真实”。

The real with its meaning read wrong and emphasis misplaced is the unreal.

我的心呀，
从世界的流动找你的美吧，
正如那小船得到风与水的优美
似的。

Find your beauty, my heart,
from the world' s movement,
like the boat that has the grace of
the wind and the water.

眼不能以视来骄人，
却以它们的眼镜来骄人。

The eyes are not proud of their
sight but of their eyeglasses.

我住在我这个小小的世界里，
生怕使它再缩小一丁点儿。把我
抬举到您的世界里去吧，
让我高高兴兴地失去我的一切的
自由。

I live in this little world of mine and am afraid to make it the least less. Life me into thy world and let me have the freedom gladly to lose my all.

虚伪永远不能凭借它生长在权力中而变成真实。

The false can never grow into truth by growing in power.

我的心，
同着它的歌，拍拍舐岸的波浪，
渴望着要抚爱这个阳光熙和的绿色世界。

My heart, with its lapping waves of son, longs to caress this green world of the sunny day.

道旁的草，
爱那天上的星吧，
你的梦境便可在花朵里实现了。

Wayside grass, love the star, then your dreams will come out in flowers.

让你的音乐如一柄利刃，
直刺入市井喧扰的心中吧。

Let your music, like a sword, pierce the noise of the market to its heart.

这树的颤动之叶，
触动着我的心，
像一个婴儿的手指。

The trembling leaves of this tree touch my heart like the fingers of an infant child.

小花睡在尘土里。
它寻求蛱蝶走的道路。

The little flower lies in the dust.It sought the path of the butterfly.

我是在道路纵横的世界上。
夜来了。打开您的门吧，
家之世界呵！

I am in the world of the roads.
The night comes. Open thy gate, thou world of the home.

我已经唱过了您白天的歌。
在黄昏的时候，
让我拿着您的灯走过风雨飘摇的道路吧。

I have sung the songs of thy day.
In the evening let me carry thy lamp through the stormy path.

我不要求你进我的屋里。
你到我无量的孤寂里来吧，
我的爱人！

I do not ask thee into the house.
Come into my infinite loneliness, my Lover.

死亡隶属于生命，
正与生一样。
举足是走路，
正如落足也是走路。

Death belongs to life as birth does.

The walk is in the raising of the foot as in the laying of it down.

我已经学会在花与阳光里微语的意义——再教我明白你在苦与死中所说的话吧。

I have learnt the simple meaning of thy whispers in flowers and sunshine — teach me to know thy words in pain and death.

夜的花朵来晚了，
当早晨吻着她时，
她战栗着，
叹息了一声，
萎落在地上了。

The night' s flower was late when the morning kissed her, she shivered and sighed and dropped to the ground.

从万物的愁苦中，
我听见了“永恒母亲”的呻吟。

Through the sadness of all things I hear the crooning of the Eternal Mother.

大地呀，
我到你岸上时是一个陌生人，
住在你屋内时是一个宾客，
离开你的门时是一个朋友。

I came to your shore as a stranger, I lived in your house as a guest, I leave your door as a friend, my earth.

当我去时，
让我的思想到你那里来，
如那夕阳的余光，
映在沉默的星天的边上。

Let my thoughts come to you, when I am gone, like the after glow of sunset at the margin of starry silence.

在我的心头燃点起那休憩的黄昏星吧，
然后让黑夜向我微语着爱情。

Light in my heart the evening star of rest and then let the night whisper to me of love.

我是一个在黑暗中的孩子。
我从夜的被单里向您伸出我的双手，母亲。

I am a child in the dark.I stretch my hands through the coverlet of night for thee, Mother.

白天的工作完了。把我的脸掩藏在您的臂间吧，母亲。
让我入梦吧。

The day of work is done.
Hide my face in your arms, Mother.
Let me dream.

集会时的灯光，
点了很久，
会散时，
灯便立刻灭了。

The lamp of meeting burns long; it goes out in a moment at the parting.

当我死时，
世界呀，
请在你的沉默中，
替我留着“我已经爱过了”这句话吧。

One word keep for me in thy silence, O World, when I am dead, I have loved.

我们热爱这个世界时，
才真正活在这个世界上。

We live in this world when we love it.

让死者有那不朽的名，
但让生者有那不朽的爱。

Let the dead have the immortality of fame, but the living the immortality of love.

我看见你，
像那半醒的婴孩在黎明的微光里，
看见他的母亲，于是微笑而又睡去了。

I have seen thee as the half-awakened child sees his mother in the dusk of the dawn and then smiles and sleeps again.

我将死了又死，
以明白生是无穷无尽的。

I shall die again and again to know that life is inexhaustible.

当我和拥挤的人群一同在路上走
过时，
我看见您从阳台上送过来的微笑。
我歌唱着，忘却了所有的喧哗。

While I was passing with the crowd in the road I saw thy smile from the balcony and I sang and forgot all noise.

爱就是充实了的生命，
正如盛满了酒的酒杯。

Love is life in its fulness like the cup with its wine.

他们点了他们自己的灯，
在他们的寺院内，
吟唱他们自己的话语。
但是小鸟们却在你的晨光中，
唱着你的名字——因为你的名字
便是快乐。

They light their own lamps and sing their own words in their temples.

But the birds sing thy name in thine own morning light, —for thy name is joy.

领我到您沉寂的中心，
使我的心充满了歌吧。

Lead me in the centre of thy silence to fill my heart with songs.

让那些选择了他们自己的焰火咝咝的世界，
就生活在那里吧。
我的心渴望着您的繁星，
我的上帝。

Let them live who choose in their own hissing world of fireworks.

My heart longs for thy stars, my God.

爱的痛苦环绕着我的一生，
像汹涌的大海似的歌唱；
而爱的快乐却像鸟儿们在花林里似的唱着。

Love's pain sang round my life like the unplumbed sea, and love's joy sang like birds in its flowering groves.

假如您愿意，
您就熄了灯吧。
我将明白您的黑暗，
而且将喜爱它。

Put out the lamp when thou wishest.

I shall know thy darkness and shall love it.

当我在那日子的终了，
站在您的面前时，
您将看见我的伤疤，
而知道我有许多的创伤，
但也有我医治的办法。

When I stand before thee at the day's end thou shalt see my scars and know that I had my wounds and also my healing.

总有一天，
我要在别的世界的晨光里对你唱
道："我以前在地球的光里，
在人的爱里，
已经见过你了。"

Some day I shall sing to thee in the sunrise of some other world,

"I have seen thee before in the light of the earth, in the love of man."

从别的日子里飘浮到我的生命里
的云，
不再落下雨点或引起风暴了，
却只给予我夕阳的天空以色彩。

Clouds come floating into my life from other days no longer to shed rain or usher storm but to give colour to my sunset sky.

真理引起了反对它自己的狂风
骤雨，
那场风雨吹散了真理广播的
种子。

Truth raises against itself the storm that scatters its seeds broadcast.

昨夜的风雨给今日的早晨戴上了
金色的和平。

The storm of the last night has crowned this morning with golden peace.

真理仿佛带了它的结论而来，
而那结论却产生了它的第二个。

Truth seems to come with its final word; and the final word gives birth to its next.

他是有福的，
因为他的名望并没有比他的真实更光亮。

Blessed is he whose fame does not outshine his truth.

您的名字的甜蜜充溢着我的心，
而我忘掉了我自己的——就像您早晨的太阳升起时，
那大雾便消失了。

Sweetness of thy name fills my heart when I forget mine — like thy morning sun when the mist is melted.

静悄悄的黑夜具有母亲的美丽，
而吵闹的白天具有孩子的美丽。

The silent night has the beauty of the mother and the clamorous day of the child.

当人微笑时，
世界爱了他；但他大笑时，
世界便怕他了。

The world loved man when he smiled. The world became afraid of him when he laughed.

神等待着人在智慧中重新获得
童年。

God waits for man to regain his childhood in wisdom.

让我感到这个世界乃是您的爱的
成形吧，
那么，
我的爱也将帮助着它。

Let me feel this world as thy love taking form, then my love will help it.

您的阳光对着我心头的冬天
微笑，
从来不怀疑它的春天的花朵。

Thy sunshine smiles upon the winter days of my heart, never doubting of its spring flowers.

神在他的爱里吻着“有涯”，
而人却吻着“无涯”。

God kisses the finite in his love and man the infinite.

您越过不毛之年的沙漠，
而到达了圆满的时刻。

Thou crossest desert lands of barren years to reach the moment of fulfilment.

神的静默使人的思想成熟而为语言。

God's silence ripens man's thoughts into speech.

“永恒的旅客”呀，
你可以在我的歌中找到你的足迹。

Thou wilt find, Eternal Traveller, marks of thy footsteps across my songs.

让我不至羞辱您吧，
父亲，
您在您的孩子们身上显出您的
光荣。

Let me not shame thee, Father, who displayest thy glory in thy children.

这一天是不快活的。光在蹙额的
云下，
如一个被打的儿童，灰白的脸上
留着泪痕；风又号叫着，似一个
受伤的世界的哭声。
但是我知道，我正跋涉着去会我
的朋友。

Cheerless is the day, the light under frowning clouds is like a punished child with traces of tears on its pale cheeks, and the cry of the wind is like the cry of a wounded world. But I know I am travelling to meet my Friend.

我梦见一颗星，
一个光明岛屿，
我将在那里出生。在它快速的闲暇深处，
我的生命将成熟它的事业，
像秋天阳光下的稻田。

I dream of a star, an island of light, where I shall be born and in the depth of its quickening leisure my life will ripen its works like the rice-field in the autumn sun.

今天晚上，
棕榈叶在嚓嚓地作响，海上有大浪，
满月呵，就像世界在心脉悸跳。
从什么不可知的天空，
您在您的沉默里带来了爱痛苦的秘密？

Tonight there is a stir among the palm leaves, a swell in the sea, Full Moon, like the heart throb of the world. From what unknown sky hast thou carried in thy silence the aching secret of love?

雨中湿土的气息，
就像从渺小的无声的群众那里来
的一阵巨大的赞美歌声。

The smell of the wet earth in the rain rises like a great chant of praise from the voiceless multitude of the insignificant.

说爱情会失去的那句话，
乃是我们不能够当作真理来接受
的一个事实。

That love can ever lose is a fact that we cannot accept as truth.

我们将有一天会明白，
死永远不能够夺去我们的灵魂所
获得的东西。因为她所获得的，
和她自己是一体。

We shall know some day that death can never rob us of that which our soul has gained, for her gains are one with herself.

神在我黄昏的微光中，
带着花到我这里来。这些花都是
我过去之时的，
在他的花篮中还保存得很新鲜。

God comes to me in the dusk of my evening with the flowers from my past kept fresh in his basket.

主呀，
当我的生之琴弦都已调得谐
和时，
你手的一弹一奏，都可以发出爱
的乐声来。

When all the strings of my life will be tuned, my Master, then at every touch of thine will come out the music of love.

让我真真实实地活着吧，
我的上帝。这样，
死对于我也就成了真实的了。

Let me live truly, my Lord, so that death to me become true.

人类的历史在很忍耐地等待着被侮辱者的胜利。

Man' s history is waiting in patience for the triumph of the insulted man.

这一刻，我感到你的眼光正落在我的心上，
像那早晨阳光中的沉默，
落在已收获的孤寂的田野上
一样。

I feel thy gaze upon my heart this moment like the sunny silence of the morning upon the lonely field whose harvest is over.

在这喧哗的波涛起伏的海中，
我渴望着咏歌之鸟。

I long for the Island of Songs across this heaving Sea of Shouts.

夜的序曲是开始于夕阳西下的
音乐，
开始于它对难以形容的黑暗，
所作的庄严的赞歌。

The prelude of the night is commenced in the music of the sunset, in its solemn hymn to the ineffable dark.

我攀登上高峰，
发现在名誉荒芜不毛的高处，
简直找不到一个遮身之地。我的
引导者呵，
领导着我在光明逝去之前，
进到沉静的山谷里去吧。在那里，
一生的收获将会成熟为黄金的
智慧。

I have scaled the peak and found no shelter in fame's bleak and barren height. Lead me, my Guide, before the light fades, into the valley of quiet where life's harvest mellows into golden wisdom.

在这个黄昏的朦胧里，
好些东西看来都仿佛是幻像一
般——尖塔的底层在黑暗里消
失了，
树顶像是墨水模糊的斑点似的。
我将等待着黎明，
而当我醒来的时候，
就会看到在光明里的您的城市。

Things look phantastic in this dimness of the dusk — the spires whose bases are lost in the dark and tree tops like blots of ink. I shall wait for the morning and wake up to see thy city in the light.

我曾经受苦过，
曾经失望过，
曾经体会过“死亡”，
于是我以我在这伟大的世界里
为乐。

I have suffered and despaired and known death and I am glad that I am in this great world.

在我的一生里，
也有贫乏和沉默的地域。它们是
我忙碌的日子得到日光与空气的
几片空旷之地。

There are tracts in my life that are bare and silent. They are the open spaces where my busy days had their light and air.

我未完成的过去，
从后边缠绕到我身上，
使我难于死去。请从它那里释放了我吧。

Release me from my unfulfilled past clinging to me from behind making death difficult.

“我相信你的爱。”让这句话做我最后的话。

Let this be my last word, that I trust thy love.

图书在版编目（CIP）数据

生如夏花：泰戈尔经典诗选：畅销百万白金纪念版.1 /（印）泰戈尔（Tagore,R.）著；郑振铎译. -- 南京：江苏凤凰文艺出版社，2016（2016.5重印）
ISBN 978-7-5399-7566-5

Ⅰ.①生… Ⅱ.①泰… ②郑… Ⅲ.①诗集 - 印度 - 现代 Ⅳ.①I351.25

中国版本图书馆CIP数据核字（2015）第301855号

书　　名	生如夏花：泰戈尔经典诗选：畅销百万白金纪念版 1
作　　者	（印）泰戈尔
译　　者	郑振铎
责任编辑	黄孝阳
出版发行	凤凰出版传媒股份有限公司 江苏凤凰文艺出版社
出版社地址	南京市中央路 165 号，邮编：210009
出版社网址	http://www.jswenyi.com
发　　行	北京时代华语图书股份有限公司　010-83670231
经　　销	凤凰出版传媒股份有限公司
印　　刷	北京中科印刷有限公司
开　　本	880×1230 毫米 1/32
印　　张	9
字　　数	128 千字
版　　次	2016 年 1 月第 1 版　2016 年 5 月第 2 次印刷
标准书号	ISBN 978-7-5399-7566-5
定　　价	39.80 元

（江苏文艺版图书凡印刷、装订错误可随时向承印厂调换）

Rabindranath Tagore
150th